STRATEGIC ALLIANCES& MARKETING
PARTNERSHIPS

Praise for *Strategic* Alliances and Marketing Partnerships

"Gibbs and Humphries have gone further than any other authors in this vexed area of 'strategic partnering'. Along the way they have exploded many myths, and got to the very essence of what works, when, and where. Their original typology of partnering types will be a vital aid to managers interested in understanding what is really happening in their supply chains, and how to address emergent issues. This is a 'must read' for those managers genuinely seeking to achieve and sustain higher levels of performance in the enterprise supply chains in which they participate."
Dr John Gattorna, author, Living Supply Chains*,*
and supply chain 'Thought Leader'

"Marketing channels are critical to our business. Understanding the dynamics of partnerships is a fundamental pre requisite. This book is invaluable in describing the complex workings of marketing channel partnerships, how to 'weigh and measure' them, identify corrective actions and crucially how to develop and manage them successfully."
Peter Ward, Vice President and General Manager, Xerox Europe

"This book explains the rational for working with marketing channels as well as the underlying dynamics of channel partnering. It is more than just a primer; it provides real insight and practical understanding to anyone whose go to market strategy embraces alliances and channels. The clarity of the explanations of complex themes and ideas is excellent, while the partnership types represent a breakthrough in our understanding of partners and how to manage and market to them."
Michel Clement, Vice President, Oracle Europe

"These boys are on to something here. We all strive to exploit our customer/supplier relationships but, human nature being what it is, we tend to move in slow and incremental steps towards our shared goals often challenged and delayed by mutual distrust and ignorance. The best take bold and imaginative steps but even they need a handrail; this book provides valuable insights into how partnerships can and should develop coherently, logically and with all stakeholders engaged, to achieve that goal of a true 'win–win' outcome."
Air Vice-Marshal Matt Wiles CBE, Director General Joint Supply Chain,
UK Ministry of Defence

STRATEGIC ALLIANCES& MARKETING PARTNERSHIPS

Gaining competitive advantage through collaboration and partnering

RICHARD GIBBS & ANDREW HUMPHRIES

RECOMMENDED BY
INSTITUTE OF DIRECTORS

KOGAN
PAGE

London and Philadelphia

Publisher's note

Every possible effort has been made to ensure that the information contained in this book is accurate at the time of going to press, and the publishers and authors cannot accept responsibility for any errors or omissions, however caused. No responsibility for loss or damage occasioned to any person acting, or refraining from action, as a result of the material in this publication can be accepted by the editor, the publisher or any of the authors.

First published in Great Britain and the United States in 2009 by Kogan Page Limited

120 Pentonville Road
London N1 9JN
United Kingdom
www.koganpage.com

525 South 4th Street, #241
Philadelphia PA 19147
USA

© Richard Gibbs and Andrew Humphries, 2009

The right of Richard Gibbs and Andrew Humphries to be identified as the author of this work has been asserted by them in accordance with the Copyright, Designs and Patents Act 1988.

ISBN 978 0 7494 5484 5

British Library Cataloguing-in-Publication Data

A CIP record for this book is available from the British Library.

Library of Congress Cataloging-in-Publication Data

Gibbs, Richard, 1955-
  Strategic alliances and marketing partnerships : gaining competitive
advantage through collaboration and partnering / Richard Gibbs and
Andrew Humphries.
      p. cm.
  Includes index.
  ISBN 978-0-7494-5484-5
  1. Strategic alliances (Business) 2. Relationship marketing. 3.
Marketing. I. Humphries, Andrew, 1949- II. Title.
  HD69.S8G53 2009
  658'.046–dc22
                                                        2008039201

Typeset by JS Typesetting Ltd, Porthcawl, Mid Glamorgan
Printed and bound in India by Replika Press Pvt Ltd

Contents

About the authors

Richard Gibbs and Andrew Humphries have a unique mix of hands-on experience and academic research and understanding.

Richard's career spans senior sales and marketing positions in major multinational companies such as Xerox and Novell Inc. Most recently he was responsible for European distribution operations at Xerox where he architected the transition from fragmented to centralized distribution services and managed the dispersed account team charged with managing established and new distributor relationships. He has also been responsible for European channel management, strategy planning and business management.

Richard's business roles are reflected in his academic interests. He has a PhD from the University of Gloucestershire where his thesis investigated the importance of relationship marketing within marketing channels and strategic alliances. Richard has an MBA from Henley Management College and is continuing his research into various aspects of inter-organizational relationships within Europe, specifically addressing how firms can gain competitive advantage through their marketing channels.

Andrew completed a 34-year career in the Royal Air Force culminating as Head of UK Defence Aviation Logistics. He founded SCCI Ltd, a company located in Milton Keynes, UK that specializes in measuring the effectiveness of and diagnosing the improvement opportunities in collaborative business relationships. His technique successfully helped to increase customer/supplier loyalty, revitalize troubled partnerships and provide performance metrics for improved governance in rail, construction, manufacturing, retail, agriculture and defence sector organizations.

Andrew gained his PhD from Cranfield School of Management and his MBA from the Open University. He continues to research the subject of collaboration between organizations and works with a number of universities in the UK and Europe. He has published widely in academic journals such as the *British Journal of Management*, the *European Journal of Marketing*, the *International Journal of Logistics Management* and the *Journal of Service Research*. He has been featured in the *Financial Times*, has written for trade and professional magazines and is a speaker at international conferences.

The authors' research programmes, which lay the foundation of this book, came together as a collaborative initiative spurred by a series of common findings and a motivation to provide operational management with a set of practical tools that will increase the likelihood of partnering excellence.

RichardKGibbs@gibbshumphries.org
AndrewHumphries@gibbshumphries.org

Foreword

This book represents the coming together of several diverse streams. Both Andrew and Richard are 'old hands' at dealing with the realities of managing major partnerships. Their extended practical experience has encompassed supply chain partners and strategic alliances as well as marketing channels in the UK, Europe and internationally. It was these experiences that led them independently to promote a better understanding of why some partnerships are more successful and more productive than others. This exploration led them into academia and a series of sizeable research programmes that enabled them to develop a deep understanding of why relationship management played such an important role in deciding the success or failure of commercial partnerships. Critically these twin research thrusts pinned down the key factors that determine partnering excellence and laid the foundation for their collaboration.

This collaboration has yielded the Gibbs+Humphries Partnership Types that are described in this book, which could potentially become the 'Myers–Briggs' equivalent to understanding business relationships. At its heart this framework helps anyone involved in partnerships gain a better appreciation of the strains and tensions that can affect them and to make more decisive decisions about how to manage them better. Their insightful review of the various theories that describe business-to-business partnering and alliances will provide the 'thinking manager' with an understanding of why and how he or she should be using the different kinds of partnering and alliances and the potential benefits they can achieve. Critically, the timing of this book could not be more appropriate. The pressures on business today to compete in a global economy force firms to work collaboratively. This is the first book that truly helps us to understand how these partnerships function and how we can manage them more effectively and efficiently.

Russell Peacock
President, North American Channels Group

Introduction:
Placing a value on
your key commercial
partnerships

The future will belong to those companies that embed alliance management capabilities into the fabric of their culture and how they do business.

(Fred Hassan, CEO Schering-Plough)

Good relationships between companies are of crucial importance. They represent the effective teamwork that allows partners and alliances to create value for customers and shareholders that could not possibly be created by individual firms. Wherever you look, you will see examples in R&D, the supply chain, marketing channels, procurement, services and manufacturing. Moreover, this collaboration is not just the preserve of the private sector; it can also be found in areas such as defence, health services and local and central government.

In response to the problems experienced by managers in understanding the dynamics within their partnerships and just how to improve their performance, this book uses marketing, supply chain and economic approaches that focus precisely on how firms work together to produce value. This combination of different concepts and ideas has been applied to answering the following critical questions:

Why are some partnerships more effective than others?
How can I predict the likely outcome of the partnership and take steps to improve its performance?

Like a comprehensive array of telemetry, it is now feasible to tap into those aspects that directly affect relationship performance and, working back from the metrics produced, see not just what is happening but also to understand why. This innovative work breaks new ground and establishes new techniques to expand knowledge in the performance of inter-organizational relationships and to provide positive benefits to firms. The synthesis of a set of key relationship drivers, a master set of probes, is cross-related to the major categories of relationship and generates the Gibbs+Humphries Partnership Types. In much the same way as Myers–Briggs explored personality types, the Gibbs+Humphries Partnership Types consider the key factors that influence how firms work together and explain the likely behaviour of each type. While it is possible to consider a myriad of such types, typically most partnerships can be categorized into one of only eight archetypal relationships, shown in Figure 0.1.

The Gibbs+Humphries Partnership Types

All animals are created equal; but some are more equal than others.

(George Orwell)

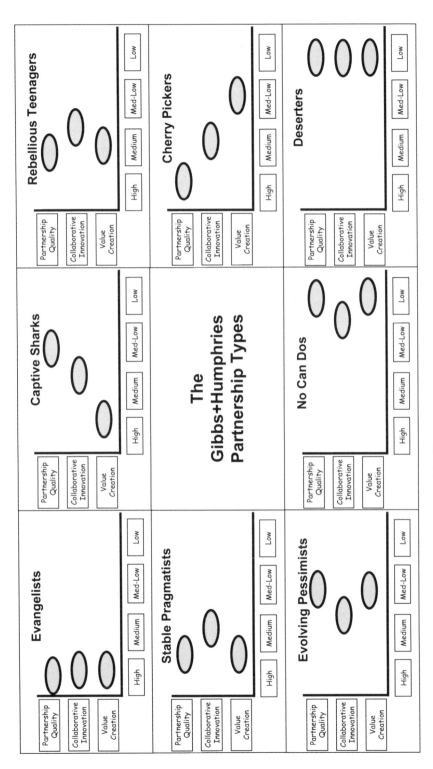

Figure 0.1 The Gibbs+Humphries Partnership Types

Understanding the Gibbs+Humphries Type of a particular partnership helps firms to manage their commercial relationships by allowing them to anticipate the potential problems and barriers to success and identify the key enablers that allow them to be leveraged. Relationship types are dissimilar to Myers–Briggs personality types in that they are not immutable; they can and do change, depending on the actions and behaviours of the participants. However, some relationship types are less malleable than others and firms are advised that the best way to deal with an immovable object is to move around it rather than go straight ahead. Other types can be transient and change subtly from one type to another over time and through the concerted efforts of both parties as they adapt to changing markets and strategies. Some Gibbs+Humphries Partnership Types are more successful than others and while there is no perfect state, firms can quickly understand what efforts should and could be made to produce the best value results given the conditions and environment.

There are eight distinctive relationship types. Each has its own distinctive characteristics, requirements and value. Understanding them helps managers to optimize their business-to-business partnerships and alliances.

Evangelists

Evangelists are firms that appear to be on an extended honeymoon for one or both of the parties involved in the partnership. The level of 'mindshare' and overall satisfaction is exceptionally high and 'word-of-mouth' references would be very positive. Quite often these are mature relationships that have become well established over time, but Evangelists can also be present among early adopters in a market or for a new product. They may also appear to be past their prime, 'living on old glories' and sceptical of change. In the early days, returns from Evangelists will be significantly above the norm but over time the benefits will tend to tail off.

Stable Pragmatists

Stable Pragmatist relationships are usually found in fairly established markets and are characterized by cooperation based upon the pragmatic need to overcome the usual supply chain operating difficulties that 'go with the territory'. Culture-matching appears to have taken place, which has brought about a feeling of 'being in the same boat'. Relationship management and relationship building are successfully embedded in the day-to-day business. On the whole, staff understand the potential benefits of cooperation and by one way or another, the partnership works. Returns from these relationships will be typically above average.

Rebellious Teenagers

Rebellious Teenager relationships are not uncommon, and often represent partnerships where the scale of contribution and performance is important to both firms. They have typically been in existence for some time, although Rebellious Teenager relationships can emerge from less mature partnerships. There is or at least has been a degree of mutual reliance in the alliance or relationship that over time is reducing and being replaced with attitudes (cultural or commercial) that are no longer wholly sympathetic to the original reasons for working together. Average returns come from these relationships but they may be subject to large 'mood-swings'.

Evolving Pessimists

Evolving Pessimist relationships exhibit many of the characteristics of No Can Dos (see below). Difficult operating conditions resulting from unstable markets and having to support complex/unreliable products are likely to preoccupy managers. These problems will affect views of the risk, and thus relationship investments in infrastructure and people will be hard to justify. Moreover, short-termist behaviours, selfishness and opportunism will tend to undermine improvement efforts. However, probably because of familiarity and prolonged experience with the operating problems, there is a certain perverse satisfaction and as a result morale has surprisingly continued to hold up. Relationship conditions may therefore have reached an unhappy truce state or at least a reduction of active adversarial behaviours. Hence, communication, especially relating to joint problem solving, will take place and marginally raise the level of innovation but, although the will to cooperate is growing, the ability to translate this into reliable product and service delivery chains has yet to develop. Returns from these relationships will be below average.

Captive Sharks

In a similar manner to Rebellious Teenagers, Captive Shark relationships often represent partnerships where the scale of contribution, performance and importance to both firms is high. It is the size of the business, the market position of the host firm or potentially contractual or market conditions that drive the relationship. The key descriptor of a Captive Shark is the very high level of commitment and dependency. This high commitment is matched by equally high levels of conflict and adversarial behaviour, which leads to low levels of collaboration. The firms are therefore hostage to the partnership and prone to act opportunistically. Returns will be below average.

Cherry Pickers

Cherry Pickers are epitomized by their lack of commitment to the relationship or dependency upon the host firm or the beneficial outcomes of the partnership. Typically they will be seen as a good and reliable partner with whom there are few major concerns or areas of conflict. Their level of overall satisfaction is also relatively high and this can confuse management into believing that growth can be anticipated. In fact these partnerships will rarely produce stellar performance; collaboration will be half-hearted and investment in the relationship low. Levels of returns will only be average as the Cherry Picker will typically be interested in short-term gains and transactional benefits.

No Can Dos

Within No Can Dos adversarial conditions are standard and since the opportunities to escape are very slim, they create strong feelings of 'imprisonment' and 'impotence'. A long-term lack of cooperation and entrenched opposition to any form of innovation also sap relationship vitality. Efforts to improve or gain better shares of the benefits are wasted. The result is poor supply chain practices and ineffective processes, often accompanied by low end-customer satisfaction and poor returns.

Deserters

While Evangelists see no 'bad' in the partnership, Deserters see no 'good'. Across all measures their assessment of the relationship is poor. No element of the partnership meets with their approval and the extent to which business aims are achieved is minimal; collaboration per se is almost non-existent. Nevertheless it should not be assumed that these firms or organizations are operating at a purely transactional level. The quality of the relationship, their experience and expectations of their partners' behaviour towards them, are important. The level of dependency and commitment is low and as their name suggests, these firms are typically most likely to desert.

Managing your commercial relationships

So, how do you decide which Gibbs+Humphries Partnership Type applies to each of your important commercial relationships? First, knowing what drives partnership success is an essential weapon in a manager's armoury. However, this is not easy. Traditionally organizations have thrived by adopting an independent, competitive culture. They have viewed commercial relationships mainly from their own angle. Customers want to 'manage' and 'develop' their suppliers. Suppliers want to extract the maximum, long-term revenues from their key accounts. Manufacturers want to leverage their marketing channels and resellers to capitalize on their capabilities. Key performance measures support these objectives by setting aggressive outcome targets such as revenue and cost reduction. However, the secret to understanding and managing your essential commercial relationships is to look at them from a 'joint' perspective; to consider leading indicators that assess not just the partnership performance (outcomes) but the firm's partnering performance. By evaluating performance jointly using the following dynamic drivers you can easily locate your partnerships in the appropriate partnership type:

- *Collaborative innovation* – the effectiveness of the relationship and the conditions that enable it to be innovative. These include responding to opportunities, through cooperation, adaptability and communication.

- *Partnership quality* – the quality of the relationship exchange based on the levels of commitment, investment, joint reliance, knowledge sharing, social bonding and trust.

- *Value creation* – the efficiency of the partnership to create and capture the potential value that the partnership offers is a sum of all the relationship-building, sustaining and developing behaviours that take place. These include operations, quality and performance management, and problem solving.

By focusing on the enablers behind each of these high-level drivers (these 'super factors') firms are able to enjoy the above-average returns that partnering excellence offers.

Metronet Rail SSL

Metronet Rail SSL was a strong company containing top-rank engineers and project managers responsible for maintaining London Underground trains and facilities. However, in 2003/4 it earned contract penalties of over £4 million. An assessment of the multi-divisional organization's collaborative capability placed it in the lower end of the Evolving Pessimists partnership type.

High-level agreement on the partners' objectives had failed to translate into guidelines for use by individuals working in a complex, multi-level interface when dealing with partners on a day-to-day basis. As a result teams worked at cross-purposes and

Metronet's over-bureaucratic organization, with its lack of clear responsibilities, led to slow and erratic problem solving. The ability to deliver operationally was further hampered by poor performance management and a lack of cohesion within its own supply chain. Thus, delivery promises were not fulfilled, people were not held to account for their failure and the firm's credibility suffered. Metronet was perceived as being an unreliable and inconsistent partner.

The poor situation made the parties wary of being open with each other for fear that information would be used to exert pressure rather than as a means of overcoming difficulties. London Underground felt that its partner was attempting to make a profit at its expense. In the face of the immense pressure to perform, Metronet Rail SSL was unable, at the same time, to overcome its internal difficulties. It ceased trading in 2007, having left understanding its partnership performance until too late.

About this book

Chapter 1 sets the scene for understanding business-to-business partnering relationships. It discusses how changes in competitive pressures have influenced the development of new organizational structures, where a firm links with other firms in inter-organizational relationships (eg, partnerships, alliances, consortia, collaborations and co-makerships) to complete its market offering. It shows how developing management ideas have reflected these changed market conditions. Chapter 1 also shows that there is growing recognition that the act of partnering and how the partnership is put into practice, rather than having partners or alliances, can make a significant contribution to a firm's performance. It describes the challenges facing people working in this highly charged and complex situation and especially those of systematically managing contract relationships. It touches on the importance of and need for performance measurement tools but, due to the difficulty of identifying the right 'levers', notes a significant lack of those specifically designed for managers to use in partnership-style relationships.

Chapter 2 discusses in detail the common types of partnerships encompassing supply chain relationships, strategic alliances, outsourcing and marketing channels. An appreciation of these structural forms is important to an understanding of the management of partnerships. This is followed in Chapter 3 by a consideration of those key features of partnerships and alliances that result in success or failure. The two, sometimes overlapping paradigms of the management of partnerships and alliances, namely economic and marketing perspectives, are explored in Chapters 4 and 5. These two very different but complementary disciplines provide rich perspectives that contribute to the development of a unique method of assessing alliance performance.

Chapters 6 and 7 describe the detailed logic of how the Gibbs+ Humphries Partnership Types are derived and built up and, more important, how they can be used to recognize the key performance issues within firms' partnership situations such that action can be taken to change them for the better. In Chapter 8 there are some practical tools that managers can use to help them decide which strategies to employ to make the necessary changes to improve the quality of their key business relationships. The chapter also shows how firms can apply the lessons learnt from the Gibbs+Humphries Partnership Types. Finally, it considers the partnership types in the context of account management and marketing as well as the product/market lifecycle, and draws out practical applications and recommendations.

At the end of each chapter some key action points are listed. If you answer the questions carefully and honestly they will build into a clear assessment of an organization's use and management of strategic commercial relationships. This will provide an understanding of those partnerships' key performance drivers and characteristic features. The review will also offer a blueprint for management action that will improve the organization's bottom line and competitive performance.

Key action points

1. How many strategically important collaborative relationships does your firm have?

2. Are you satisfied with their performance?

3. What measures do you use to evaluate the performance of your partnerships?

4. What measures do you use to evaluate the quality of your partnering?

5. Do your current KPIs give you the information and confidence to manage these partnerships effectively?

6. Would they give you enough time to act if a relationship were going wrong?

1 The business of partnering

Partnering is no longer a part of our business; it is our business.

(Peter Ward, Vice President and General Manager, Xerox Europe)

A crisis in management

The Ford Motor Company in the 1930s epitomized the then-prevalent image of a highly successful, profitable and dynamic business. Its River Rouge plant that manufactured the Model A Ford characterized the fully integrated firm that produced a single standardized product. But it wasn't only a manufacturing unit; the Ford Motor Company was a large firm and by definition this meant that it was well positioned to do everything for itself, with little or no need for outside contracting.

From its own mines Ford produced iron and coal which it transported on its own lake steamships that were docked at one end of the plant. Heat for the treatment and paint ovens came from gases from the coking ovens. The moulds for parts were filled with molten iron from its blast furnaces. Sawdust and shavings from the body shop together with the waste gases from the blast furnaces became fuel for the power plant boilers. For the interior of the car, Ford could use wool from its own sheep farms and rubber from its plantations and then transport materials from site to site on its own railway. This was scale, this was productivity, this was the fully integrated firm. However, in 2006 Bill Ford, Executive Chairman, in an e-mail to all Ford employees, wrote, 'The business model that sustained us for decades is no longer sufficient to sustain profitability.'

Anne Mulcahy, CEO of Xerox, grew up in the firm when, according to her, it had three channels of distribution: 'direct, direct and direct'. Under her leadership Xerox has embraced the mantra of 'partner or perish' and expanded its indirect marketing coverage through the acquisition of Tektronix, Global Imaging Systems and Veenman.

Traditional business models that were stable for decades are now being forced to change rapidly. After periods of downsizing, right-sizing and business process reengineering, any further reductions in costs have been countered by diminishing returns and concerns over quality, employee motivation and retention. Moreover, new pressures have developed. Marketing and sales battles against global competition and shortened product lifecycles. Marginal product advantages in many markets have demonstrated all the hallmarks of commoditization. Meanwhile, the challenge of meeting customers' expectations has become tougher as their market knowledge has grown, due in great part to the internet. Their loyalty has also become even harder to secure as they seek to satisfy ever more complex and sophisticated needs in trends that are difficult to identify and track. Many CEOs have been forced to concentrate on top-line revenue growth and simultaneously earnings per share because the ever-persistent stock markets are looking over their shoulders every quarter for signs of balance sheet weakness. From within this maelstrom, firms are desperately looking for ways to develop a sustainable, competitive advantage.

In the 21st century the strategy discussion has re-awoken to the critical importance of firms working with other firms. Whether under the banner of the networked firm, the extended enterprise, strategic alliance, the more academic-sounding 'inter-organizational relationships' or simply partnering, firms are looking to gain competitive advantage through collaborative initiatives.

The focus has intensified over the last 10 years as more and more senior managers have recognized that they can no longer 'go it alone' to fulfil the demands of the sophisticated customer. Upwards of 50 per cent of the total Fortune 1000 revenue can be attributed to alliances, marketing channels or other collaborative activities. Partnering or outsourcing to reduce costs is well understood, but firms are now finding that collaboration in the form of external partnering can also bring major tangible strategic and competitive benefits if correctly managed. These benefits are translatable into balance sheet and P&L performance gains; for example, firms that perform higher in terms of gross operating margin are the same organizations that collaborate more extensively. Revenue growth for successful collaborators is also more than twice that of less collaborative firms.

The demands of the marketplace, the scale of business generated through partnering, and the benefits from successful collaboration now underline the essentiality of the business of partnering. Partnering has thus moved to become a central plank of many firms' strategy and a key building block in the new-order business models which are being crafted and adopted.

Diminishing sources of competitive advantage

Constant reinvention is the central necessity at GE... We're all just a moment away from commodity hell.

(Jeffrey Immelt, Chairman and CEO, GE)

Whether or not you consider the world to be flat like Thomas Friedman or spiky like Richard Florida, it certainly has a radically different geography to the one you were taught at school. The world has changed and the forces that have driven that change are not stopping; in fact, they are gaining momentum.

Over a decade ago, management theorists were pointing to the accelerated pace of technological change as a critical factor impacting company strategy. Each new development offered the opportunity for differentiation but it was confronted by an almost immediate response from competitors offering greater functionality, frequently at a reduced price. The net result was that product development in many areas became a question of catch-up and leapfrog, as each new innovation edged capabilities further along but did not provide a sustainable advantage. The cost of new product development increased simultaneously with R&D budgets being squeezed, if not reduced. Time to market became crucial for firms simply because being able to offer a functionally competitive product meant that you were either in the game or out, effectively for good. Thus development timelines were shortened and so were product lifecycles. These shortened product lifecycles had financial implications as well. The break-even point had to be brought forward. In fact products were often put on the market in the knowledge that they would be unprofitable, simply to ensure that market share was maintained. This behaviour was bound to run out of steam.

The Berlin Wall fell in 1989 heralding the end of the Cold War, and the subsequent expansion of the European market created a new, substantial economic entity of 27 states which in 2007 generated an estimated 31 per cent share of the world's nominal GDP. In the 1990s the four Asian Tigers – South Korea, Singapore, Hong Kong and Taiwan – made the majority of the economic 'running' in the Far East region. However, new 'tigers' have emerged. The transfer of sovereignty of Hong Kong to the People's Republic of China in 1997, the entry of China into the World Trade Organization in 2001 and the 2008 Beijing Olympic Games have signalled the opening up of the Chinese market to the rest of the world. Progress has been very rapid with the achievement of huge improvements in quality and technological capacity as well as reduced complexity and cost. The other emergent country has been India. With the opening up of its markets in 1991 by Manmohan Singh, the former Indian Finance Minister, India now represents the strategic hot-house of the world's technology companies. Silicon Valley has now spiritually relocated to Bangalore.

Business people across a wide range of industries have increasingly begun to identify maturity and commoditization as serious, emerging challenges. Whether due to globalization, maturing technologies, ease of imitation, decreasing barriers to entry, open standards in technology markets or pressures from customers who are themselves being squeezed, companies are feeling more and more the intensity of price competition. As a result, firms have been forced to look elsewhere for competitive advantage.

From product-base competition to knowledge-base advantage

The market forces that have created successes like Google, taken us through the dot com bubble and forced regeneration on erstwhile behemoths like Ford and Xerox, have been reflected in different management theories on business and strategy. Two schools of thought infuse the discussions of how firms achieve competitive advantage, one with an external focus, the other internal.

Most MBA textbooks will start with Michael Porter's seminal ideas on the impact that industry structure has on determining a firm's ability to earn above-average profits. Porter's approach characterized traditional market economics with its heavy reliance on the assessment of the competitive environment through a SWOT analysis. The numbers of competitors, the scale of investment needed to participate in the business and the density of customers were factors that could influence a market's profitability. In his book *Competitive Strategy: Techniques for analyzing industries and competitors,* first published in 1980, Porter simplified business strategies into three generic options: cost leadership, differentiation and market segmentation (or focus). However, all of this rested on two basic assumptions: that the marketplace could be defined within specified boundaries and that firms were effectively homogeneous entities in terms of capacity and capabilities.

Today the complexity of the product-market situation is exemplified by the Apple iPhone. In 1997 mobile phone unit sales totalled just over 100 million, and in June 2007 Apple launched the iPhone. The new product represented a significant change in Apple's strategic approach, moving outside of the strict confines of the computer into the broader realms of consumer electronics and digitally connected lifestyles. In 1997 mobile phones had evolved only slightly beyond their brick or lunchbox designs. Today the technology is being subsumed into a lifestyle accoutrement with service offerings going well beyond telecommunications and substantial profits coming from the sale of downloaded music and videos. The mobile phone market in general has exploded, but for the iPhone, Apple forecast relatively modest sales of 10 million units by the end of 2008, which would translate into an approximate 1 per cent share of the world market for handsets. Even before the iPhone was launched, the market was already discussing the next concept, the upgrades that would follow and the competitor products from firms such as Sony that would attempt to take the edge off the iPhone launch and constrain its growth and dominance. Since its launch, rivals have emerged from Sony, Nokia, Motorola, RIM and others as the communication market crashes into the entertainment market and radically impacts the music industry.

As globalization and product commoditization became more prevalent, an alternative school of thought emerged that adopted a different perspective. This shifted the focus away from an external analysis to an internal appraisal of the firm's ability to use what it has (resources and capabilities) in such a way as to outperform its competitors. Two of the main originators of this internalized focus were C K Prahalad and Gary Hamel.

Resources (bundles of assets) are the source of an organization's capabilities (how well it makes use of its assets) and determine the difference in performance between one firm and another. Resources are considered as the tradable, generic assets that can be divided into three: tangible (infrastructure, natural resources and money), intangible (image, reputation, markets and brands) and human (experts).

Capabilities are distinctive and unique to the firm (organizing, R&D, selling and team-working abilities). They are developed over time and take considerable care and acumen to amass and leverage. For a capability to be 'distinctive' it must be hard to imitate and will involve drawing on combinations of resources from all parts of the organization and also from those that may be outsourced or networked. Strategic management thus extends into HR, financial management, organizational development, technology development and implementation, to create unique bundles of capabilities from across the broadest spectrum of the firm's interests. Against internal and external conditions of uncertainty, complexity and conflict, managerial expertise is applied to creating and deploying this mix as a sustainable source of advantage for the firm.

Initially there was an upsurge in patents (registration and litigation) as firms sought to document and protect their potential advantages. This was followed by cross-licensing arrangements between firms that spurred new sectors such as 'edutainment' (education + entertainment) as well as reinvigorating the PC market and creating lifestyle technology (epitomized by the iPhone and of course the iPod). Firms were now recognizing the benefits of working together to build and create value into their product offerings to avoid 'commodity hell'.

Extending the boundaries of the firm

From the 1850s to the 1950s firms of ever increasing size and complexity typified business. It was only in the 1980s that new organizational structures were seen to be emerging that were based less on vertical integration and market-based processes and more on administrative processes and negotiation.

Airbus

It was during this period that Airbus Industries emerged as a consortium that reflected these strategic and organizational trends. The charter of Airbus Industries was to provide a credible European competitor to US companies such as Boeing, McDonnell Douglas and Lockheed. European aircraft manufacturing was fragmented and competition was fuelled by national interests that left them as expensive, light-weight contenders against the agile US heavy-weights. In the mid-1960s, tentative negotiations began regarding a European, collaborative approach where capital costs could be shared and know-how traded upon. It would take the better part of a decade for the alliance to become an effective force, by which time it comprised French, German, Spanish and British companies all charged with manufacturing elements of the Airbus 300 – the world's first twin-engined, wide-bodied passenger aircraft.

Despite many setbacks, internal disagreements and governmental interference, the A300 made its maiden flight in 1972 and entered commercial service in 1974. The A300 was not an overnight success but the launch of the A320 in 1981 firmly established Airbus as a major player in the aircraft market. By 2007 Airbus had 'morphed' into a joint venture that now employs around 57,000 people at 16 sites in four European countries. It has also, despite considerable hardships and internal turmoil, launched the Airbus A380, which seats 845 passengers and is the world's largest commercial passenger jet. Since its launch the A380 has endured continuing and troublesome delays in delivery, which have particularly impacted the freight version known as the A380F.

There was a parallel trend that saw firms looking to gain additional competences from outside of their own staff, either to round off their offering or to create something entirely new. In the 1990s, Benetton was the archetypal exponent of creating a value chain of capabilities. Its manufacturers were all part-time, contracted out, and its retailers were mainly franchises. Benetton provided the just-in-time logistics system, the garment finishing/warehousing, the branding/market positioning and advertising as well as pioneering use of EPOS-fed information systems. This proved to be a winning combination that was, at the time, very hard to imitate. Today, Nike Inc, the United States-based sports company, is a prime example of the virtual enterprise where information systems are used to coordinate each step of its far-flung activities, from material sourcing and manufacturing through to marketing and retailing. This coming together of firms into inter-organizational relationships, whether strategic alliances or partnerships, outsourcing or co-manufacturing, can be seen as a direct reaction to the changing market conditions that have been described.

Oliver Williamson's 'transaction cost economics' ideas constitute one of the most important management paradigms that explain the reasons for this phenomenon and helps us to understand the mechanics of firms working collaboratively. As firms look at ways to reduce or strip out costs from their business, an analysis of the value chain reveals that certain primary activities are key to the business; these are its competences. Where the firm has a unique capacity or capability it makes sense to continue to keep this in-house. But where the activity is less central to the business an evaluation can be made as to whether it is more cost-effective to engage a third party to perform the task. This is the 'make or buy' decision that many firms call 'investment appraisal'. It is also the basis of transaction cost economics theory but, importantly, TCE takes a wider view of costing into consideration.

One important element is the cost to the firm of coordinating or managing the activity in-house compared to buying it in. In this sense the external costs include negotiating, contracting and controlling the activity of ordering and acquiring these goods or services from the market. These are known as 'transaction costs'. Internally these costs are associated with the learning, organization and management of the activity such as design and production. Williamson did not limit himself to a purely economic view of costs. He also considered the management costs and risks associated with the people involved. His ideas did not give personnel (your own or partner's) much credit for trustworthiness. He believed that it was inevitable that individuals would look for opportunities to take advantage of the organization or other people; it was the naturally competitive thing to expect and necessarily carried a management cost.

Management costs are therefore a significant part of the equation, whether it is drawing up contracts or organizational safeguards such as compliance departments. Notwithstanding the above, a further means of reducing the tendencies of firms to act selfishly is by both parties investing in their relationships by contributing, for example, know-how, time and infrastructure. These non-returnable (sunk) investments build commitment and loyalty and establish a longer-term attitude to the alliance and, of course, represent some of the additional aspects of the broader economic cost equation. In summary, therefore, where these transaction costs are high relative to production costs, firms will carry out the activity in-house, and vice versa. Accordingly, a firm should undertake activities that it can perform at a lower cost, and outsource other activities to the market for additional advantage.

This trend to outsourcing was greatly helped by the increasing sophistication and capabilities of information technology. IT functionality enabled far greater and easier control of the distributed operation, and soon 'outsourcing' became 'off- shoring' as firms saw back-office functions as well as assembly and manufacturing relocated to lower-cost parts of the world. Despite the geographic dispersal of key functions, firms were able to establish strict control mechanisms in the form of contracts and service level agreements to ensure their requirements were met. Regular review meetings supported by the real-time data from computer-regulated manufacturing and other systems allowed the examination of specified metrics to weigh and measure the performance of the supplier. Nevertheless, disappointments and disagreements were frequent and often well publicized. Many of the gains of outsourcing have thus been unrealized and over 50 per cent of arrangements seem to have failed within three years. A critical factor for many of these failures was often the scale of management effort required to command and control such operations, which was underestimated or not understood. This reinforces Williamson's original thinking and points us in the direction of needing to consider in more detail the broader, non-economic factors involved in partnering, alliances and outsourcing in order to ensure successful delivery of our objectives.

The strategic value of partnering

To address the challenges of a radically different marketplace, firms are recognizing the need for successful partnerships and the benefits they bring. Some of these factors are shown in Figure 1.1.

Companies will engage in some form of partnership or alliance relationship for a number of persuasive reasons. They may wish to overcome a weakness (for example, low performance or high cost) in the resources available to them and to establish or recreate a competitive position. They may look to acquire new skills and gain new competences through inter-organizational learning, and then to exploit these beyond the confines of the original partnerships or relationships to provide them with market advantages. On a broader front they may also seek to gain approval and status from

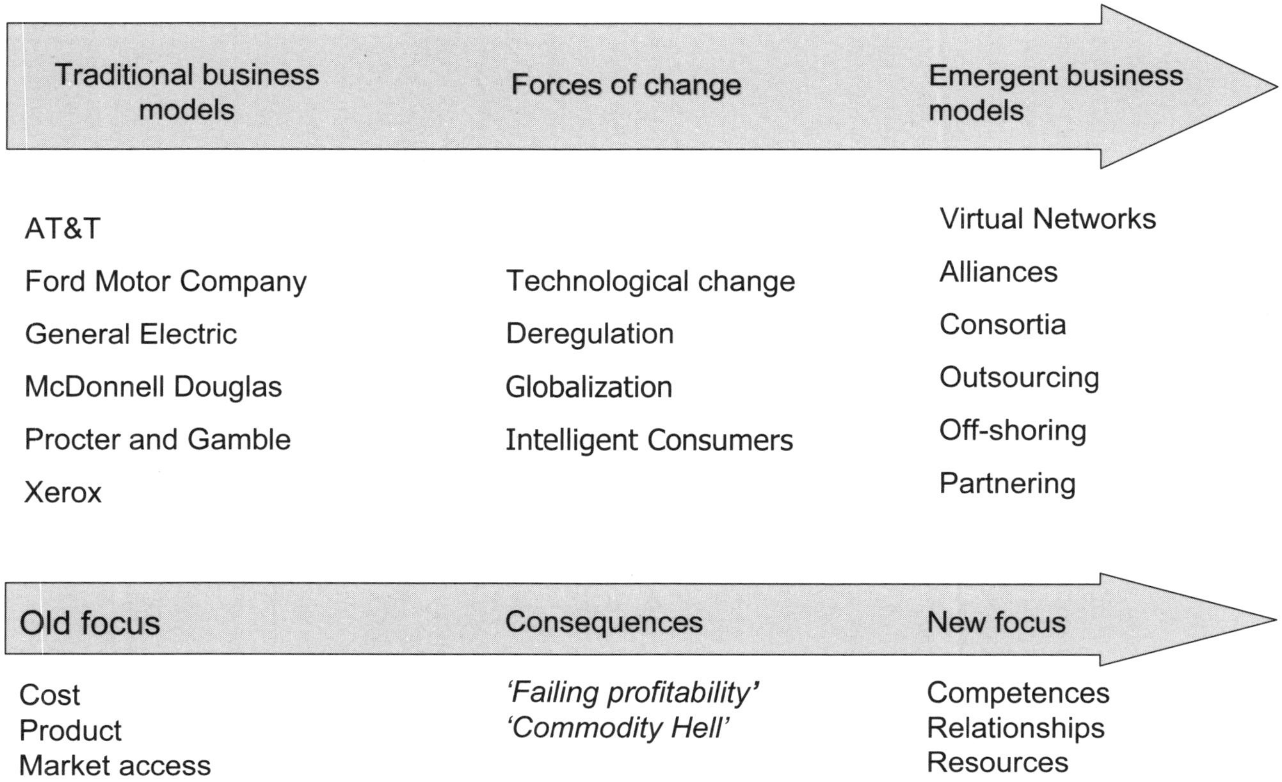

Traditional business models

AT&T
Ford Motor Company
General Electric
McDonnell Douglas
Procter and Gamble
Xerox

Forces of change

Technological change
Deregulation
Globalization
Intelligent Consumers

Emergent business models

Virtual Networks
Alliances
Consortia
Outsourcing
Off-shoring
Partnering

Old focus

Cost
Product
Market access

Consequences

'Failing profitability'
'Commodity Hell'

New focus

Competences
Relationships
Resources

Figure 1.1 The factors that drive organizations to partner

within an industry by joining up with a more prestigious or powerful organization. Of course they may simply be seeking improved market share growth and sales performance through collaboration and joint working. Partnerships can also enable firms to create new customer values through the synergistic combination of previously separate resources, creating new innovative solutions and products that singly no one firm could offer. Or firms could turn to partnering to neutralize common competitive threats by combining resources to create scale and muscle, as exemplified in the Airbus consortium.

Two academics at the forefront of partnering theory and understanding, Doz and Hamel, consider six strategic logics for entering into partnerships. Each logic can be identified and each can stand up to inspection as the sole rationale for exploiting a relationship, but typically more than one will be present in any given situation. These are shown in Figure 1.2 and explained below.

Building critical mass

There are many good examples of how entering into tense markets through partnering can circumvent Michael Porter's barriers to entry. First, the liberalization of the European telecommunications market in the late 1990s encouraged Deutsche Telekom and France Telecom into a collaborative alliance with the 'deep pockets' and breadth of resources to compete effectively against the giant US AT&T organization. Secondly, NTT DoCoMo in Japan, a regional mobile telephone carrier, launched its mobile access to the internet service called i-mode. DoCoMo was able to gain a 45 per cent penetration of the Japanese market for cellular phones by partnering with content providers as opposed to creating it itself. This enabled DoCoMo to quickly offer its customers a critical mass of services and content that gave it a key edge over its competition.

Reaching new markets

While the usage of marketing channels is sometimes reduced to a simple question of variable sales cost, major benefits can accrue to firms that expand their market reach through intermediaries. Novell was a small Utah-based networking company in the 1980s. Its

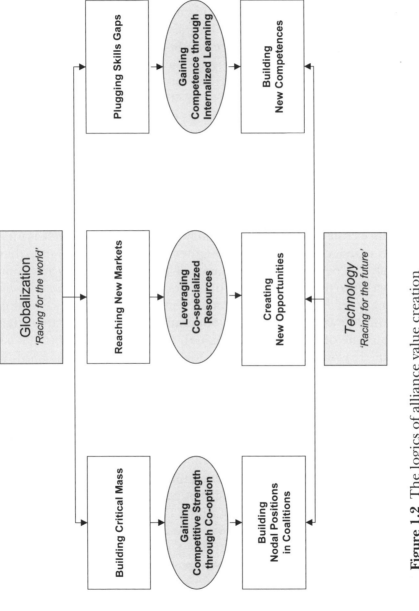

Figure 1.2 The logics of alliance value creation

product was functionally above average, if liable to 'flakiness', but its major weakness was its inability to compete with the market coverage that the (then) wholly direct IBM and Digital (DEC) could muster. However, it recognized that it could compete most effectively in the fragmented small and medium business sector. The challenge was how it could engage with the large number of customers in this market segment. The answer was to engage local value-added resellers, to train and accredit them and nurture and develop them to the extent that Steve Ballmer, then President of Microsoft, opined that Novell had 'more partners than 7-eleven: it's easier to buy Netware than it is to get a Big Gulp'.

Building new competences

As technological change becomes pervasive, and firms have sought to reduce costs and increase efficiency by using methods such as total quality management, process reengineering and lean six sigma, they have also recognized the importance of bringing new skills and competences into the organization. In his book *The Fifth Discipline: The art and practice of the learning organization,* Peter Senge defined a learning organization as human beings cooperating in dynamic systems that are in a state of continuous adaptation and improvement.

A key reason often overlooked for entering into partnerships is the learning that can be acquired from the partner. One of the most successful 'learning alliances' has been between Xerox Corporation and Fuji Photo Film Co. Fuji Xerox Co Ltd was established in 1962 as a 50:50 partnership and initially enabled Xerox to gain access to the lucrative Japanese market. But the real benefit was even more significant. As Xerox entered one of its darker periods in the 1980s, senior executives visiting Japan noted the focus on quality and quality tools. Through learning from Fuji Xerox, Xerox was able to redefine itself as a high quality company. Since 1980, Xerox and Fuji Xerox have won 25 national quality awards in 20 countries, including the world's three most prestigious. In the United States, Xerox is a two-time winner of the Malcolm Baldrige National Quality Award: for Xerox Business Services in 1997 and for Xerox Business Products and Systems in 1989. Xerox Europe, formerly Rank Xerox, won the first European Quality Award in 1992. Fuji Xerox won the Deming Prize, Japan's highest and most prestigious quality award, in 1980. All of this enabled Xerox to withstand immense competitive pressure following the loss of key patents and growing price competition.

Plugging skills gaps

Many organizations will support continuous learning programmes. There is a general recognition that reliance on old skills and method-ologies does not equip firms to compete in the new era that is unfolding as you read this. Being able to utilize the latest technology that saves costs in the back office or adopt a new approach that reduces time to market are critical requirements for many firms. There is a point, however, where a firm recognizes that either it can-not keep pace with this constant change or that the acquisition of new capabilities takes it too far outside its own core competences. In these instances firms will turn to outside service providers, often in the form of an outsourcing arrangement, whose specialized skills substitute for the firms' deficiencies. These outsourced facilities enable firms to leverage all the advanced technology and economies of scale of the provider without needing to step outside of their sphere of competence or experience or to make significant investment in capital.

Building nodal positions in coalitions

Coalitions can often lead to strange bedfellows and this may be characterized by 'co-opetition'. Co-opetition is the concept of co-operation taking place between firms that would otherwise be in com-petition with one another. Co-opetition enables a firm to strategically manage its potential competitor, either directly or by ensuring that a potential competitive coalition is stalled or circumvented. This was how JVC won the 'VCR war' against Betamax in the 1970s. Betamax was generally regarded as a superior product in most respects, but JVC was able to position VHS as the dominant standard through a strategy of co-opetition and coalition. The central tenets of this strategy were the creation of coalitions with RCA in the United States and Thomson in Europe, which could have easily joined with Philips and endorsed Betamax. RCA and Thomson brought with them their major distribution coverage that enabled VHS to move a large volume of products into the market, which gained rapid consumer acceptance, spurred the growth of video rental and became the subsequent de facto standard.

Creating new opportunities

Whether it is a new pharmaceutical drug or entrance into a new geographic territory, partnerships can pave the way for sharing costs, risks and expertise, especially under conditions of uncertainty. Alliances are playing an increasingly important role in innovation. They help firms to scan their environment for promising new technologies at a lower cost than doing so in isolation, and make it possible for a firm to get a 'sneak preview' of a variety of technological opportunities without fully committing to them.

For fresh, new opportunities, consider the combination of Mercedes cars and fashion accessory Swatch watches to produce the Smart car, or the electronic skills of Philips matched with the capability of Douwe Egberts to produce the SenseoCream coffee machine. These are instances of innovative hybridization where two streams of technology come together to form a radically new concept and product. Both parties recognize that the unique combination of skills and resources can not only create a new opportunity but, critically, give them a significant first-mover advantage. And in terms of pure R&D consider Xerox Parc, the source of much of what is taken for granted on the PC (from graphical interfaces to ethernet) which now has a multi-year relationship with Fujitsu and an entrance into biomedical sciences in partnership with the Scripps Research Institute of La Jolla, California.

Partnering and competing supply chains.

All-pervasive business pressures including scarcity of resources, increased competition, globalization of markets, faster change and higher customer expectations have resulted in an increase in external focus and vertical 'disintegration' as companies have out-sourced non-core activities This has led to a concentration on improving operational efficiency in the supply chain through the adoption of just-in-time supply and a recognition of the necessary contribution of other third parties. In turn this has created a plethora of coordinated process initiatives, both up and down the channels of supply and distribution. These process initiatives have led to an extended view of supply chains to include multi-organizational networks, value webs, coordinated collectives and industry-spanning entities (at the same time spawning a whole new vocabulary). All of this has the prime intention of reducing inter-functional costs – especially inventory holdings.

The ability to gain flexibility through agility and to achieve lean supply through the 'quasi-firm' means that supply chain innovation continues to adopt more integrated and holistic approaches. Furthermore, the pace of change is affected by the realization that customer service directly results from the combined efforts of all the supply chain organizations. This is known as 'demand chain management', which is able to provide a unique type of value to customers. Latterly, John Gattorna's concept of 'dynamic supply chain alignment' has entered the fray. This focuses on matching changing customer needs and desires to different supply chain strategies. It requires a firm to segment its different customers and then to tailor its service offering accordingly. The result is continuous replenishment supply chains where customers and suppliers are truly collaborative and all parties, including third-party logistics providers, work together to lower costs, meet demand and continuously improve delivery times and service. In the public sector, demands for improved value for money and sustainability have been the principal drivers for change and have brought about a similarly radical review of the role and conduct of supply chain relationships.

Supply chain relationships have been described as enduring transaction flows and linkages that come about for a variety of reasons. These include 'necessity' in, for example, a defence monopoly situation where there is only one buyer and one manufacturer for a particular product, and 'asymmetry' where a dominant partner insists on supply chain integration. Pfizer, the pharmaceutical company, insists that its suppliers conform to its supply chain management standards. To highlight the strategic nature of these collaborative buyer-seller relationships they have been called 'co-destiny' situations where the parties are inextricably linked. Partnerships are defined as demand-led, integrated, inter-company relationships based on collaboration that is long-term and focused on complex problem solving. They involve tailored business arrangements based on mutual trust, openness, shared risks and rewards that leverage the skills of each partner to achieve competitive performance not achieved by individual partners. This has been termed 'co-makership' because it represents a seamless, end-to-end pipeline or virtual corporation between the supplier and the customer. It is based on high-quality processes, cooperation, interdependence, openness, trust, commitment, shared goals, open information flows and long-term mutual benefits. Moreover, in such partnerships, customers and suppliers commit to continuous improvement and shared benefits by exchanging information openly and resolving problems by working together. In turn, they are able to harness the unique capabilities of partnership that make it possible to protect their joint enterprise from 'surprises' in tough, global markets. Illustrative of this change of approach is the way that the manufacturer aims to reduce a supplier's costs, not its profits, through process improvements. Through collaboration and closely integrated logistics planning systems, the partners seek to achieve a 'win–win' outcome. Major companies in the UK such as Masterfoods and Nissan have proved this is eminently possible.

Commercial pressures have therefore moved the supply chain from the dark days of lowest cost procurement to collaborative, complex and integrated teams. The US automotive industry, for example, is typically characterized by testosterone-fuelled negotiations, but under the charismatic leadership of Tom Stallkamp, Chrysler changed the rules (at least until its acquisition by Daimler). Chrysler's SCORE programme developed closer working relationships with its suppliers, incentivized them for their performance, shared cost savings with them and brought them generally closer into the production and development activities. The savings that SCORE generated for Chrysler amounted to billions of dollars over an extended period of time.

The white goods manufacturer Whirlpool attributes improvements in productivity and the success of its new product development to closer working relationships with its supplier base. This closer working partnership is conditioned by a level of trust and the recognition of common goals that enable global advantages to be obtained from within the highly competitive white goods market, with its slim margins.

The ability to construct and manage the highly complex webs of relationships that form supply chains is a significant competitive advantage because it is clear that supply chains are strategic capabilities that underpin firms' ability to deliver value to their customers. Martin Christopher, an innovative thinker and inventor of the term 'marketing logistics', declared that in today's environment, 'supply chains compete, not firms' and that it is no longer one firm's product compared to another's, but the whole interconnected supply chain that is in competition. Understanding how to do this better than your competitors is thus a market-winning competence.

The problems of understanding your partners

Two strategic approaches, when properly combined, allow managers to leverage their company's skills and resources well beyond levels available in other strategies. First, concentrate the firm's own resources on a set of 'core competences' where it can achieve definable pre-eminence and provide unique value to customers. Secondly, strategically outsource other activities – including many traditionally considered integral to any company – for which the firm has neither a critical strategic need nor special capabilities. The combination of its own core competencies and those provided through its partnerships with other firms creates value to the extent that a firm's competitive position is defined by a collection of unique resources and relationships. This leads to the proposition that strategic alliances become a primary tool in developing a firm's core competence and competitive advantage, and that this can be extended to include other forms of inter-organizational relationships. Given the above, it is clear that these partnerships are resources available to the firm and as such can be considered as strategically important to the extent that they can make a substantial contribution to its overall financial performance.

But partnerships in themselves as corporate assets are insufficient. It is known that upwards of 70 per cent of all strategic alliances in the 1990s failed to deliver on their objectives or to live up to expectations of their potential. Any asset needs to be utilized and leveraged through the capabilities or competences of the firm such that it can bring about the performance gain or positively affect the investment analysts' valuation of the firm. What therefore becomes important is not so much the partnership itself and the agreement or the memorandum of understanding between two firms, but the manner in which it is managed and exploited.

This chapter has shown how market pressures have forced firms to adopt cooperative strategies around partnering and how these can be established on the basis of six strategic logics that encompass market coverage activities as well as joint R&D initiatives. The crucial part that supply chains play in a firm's competitive strategy and how it has moved from the recent dark ages to a more enlightened management philosophy has been demonstrated. It is thus a surprising fact that many commercial relationships do not achieve their full potential. Managers have traditionally focused on operational efficiency and have tended to embrace partnerships only when process cost-saving initiatives have reached diminishing returns. This 'port of last resort' mentality is now changing, but firms continue to engage in partnerships with a bullishness that sets an adversarial tone.

Relational dealings in contrast are characterized by fewer, longer-term contracts that require deeper involvement and cultural adjustments to achieve success. Rather than looking over a defined, and often entrenched, boundary at each other, firms have to consider mutual goals, joint performance measures, formal information and communication system linkages, C3 (cooperation, coordination and collaboration) and softer issues such as building trust and commitment. The task of managing collaborative contracts is more time-consuming, difficult and specialized than the 'choreography' of internal, organization processes, a fact that was realized by Oliver Williamson in his 'make or buy' ideas.

The established techniques of supplier relationship management (SRM), with the emphasis on time, cost and quality, fall short in delivering real value under the demands of complex relationship management. Often this situation is exacerbated when faced by a partner that is using key account management (KAM) strategies to obtain the highest rates of return from its strategic customers. These self-centred approaches are culturally and functionally incompatible. Account management carried out from separate, entrenched positions will not deliver the potential for which the alliance was originally established, ie the creation of value that both partners could not generate individually.

Traditional management techniques are nevertheless insufficient to extract the best performance from supply chain and marketing channel relationships. Centralized relationship management needs to be underpinned by objective performance measurement that will provide the appropriate knowledge necessary to monitor, steer and improve partnership activities. Such performance metrics should be used to seek out areas for corrective action and not simply form the basis for punitive actions.

Unfortunately, commonly used financial measures, quality systems and balanced scorecard methods are not designed to 'tap' the complex cocktail of inter-organizational, operational and interpersonal dynamics when applied to one-to-one, one-to-many and many-to-many relationship configurations. Any attempt to use these traditional approaches typically results in little gain or benefit, and frequently a negative view of the 'expensive and manipulative' partners.

Many studies have been carried out involving considerable amounts of theoretical modelling. But, because of the practical difficulties of researching pairs or networks of relationships and the large number of dynamics at play, most of the projects have been generic (eg, asking managers to comment generally on their business relationships) or very granular and detailed (examining the effects of communication flows on respective power positions). As a result, very little has been revealed about partnership performance from an integrated and multi-party perspective. Therefore until now there has been a dearth of useful tools to support managers who are struggling with the practical complexities of managing strategically important partnering relationships on a day-to-day basis.

Key action points

1. What are the industry-level changes that have impacted your firm's business model in the last 5 to 10 years?

2. To what extent are your competitors today the same competitors as five years ago?

3. How has your firm's business model altered in the last 5 to 10 years?

4. How will your firm's business model alter in the next 5 to 10 years?

5. What initiatives has your company undertaken to maintain/ enhance its competitive position in the marketplace?

6. In which of the following would you see the strategic advantage of your firm lying:
   - manufacturing prowess;
   - engineering and product development;
   - access to market and customers;
   - skills and competences;
   - financial structure of the business;
   - reputation and credibility;
   - processes and/or patents;
   - IM systems and structure;
   - upstream supply chain arrangements with suppliers and outsourcing arrangements;
   - downstream 'go to market' arrangements with distributors and intermediaries?

7. Considering one or more of your partnering arrangements, what is the strategic logic(s) that underpins the relationship?

8. What percentage of your firm's total revenue can be attributed to working with upstream and downstream partners?

9. How adversarial are your negotiations with your supply chain partners?

10. To what extent do your IT systems interface directly with those of your suppliers, logistic providers or other outsource arrangements?

11. How does your firm's corporate positioning reflect the idea that 'supply chains compete, not firms'?

12. How do you measure success in your partnerships today?

13. How do you manage for success in your partnerships today?

14. Are your performance measures the same measures used to manage the relationship?

2 The evolution of partnership-driven business strategies

If you think you can go it alone in today's global economy, you are highly mistaken.

(Jack Welch, CEO, General Electric)

Introduction

Chapter 1 emphasized the importance of firms operating a partnering strategy. This chapter focuses on the development of business relationships within the supply chain and marketing channels. It concentrates on these areas because they provide pragmatic and operational perspectives that managers will find useful when seeking solutions to their own alliance issues.

It is clear from the general business language that close relationships between organizations can be defined in a plethora of ways, because partnering is now such a common strategy in both the private and public sectors. Companies have significantly reduced the number of contracts they manage and those they do have are closer, longer-term and characterized by greater teamwork and trust. It is also likely that firms will have a portfolio of contractual relationships that they may have initiated separately or in combination. It is probable they will take different forms and structures such as supply chain partnerships, strategic alliances, manufacturer/intermediary partnerships, buyer/seller relationships and consortia for R&D and other purposes. However, their general features are likely to include transactions that are frequent and repeated, relationship managers who are employed to provide an interface to the firm, and business performance being measured over time.

This chapter describes the development of business-to-business relationship strategies, their variations and configurations, the reasons for their formation and their management challenges. It shows how they are able to generate superior, long-term returns and how many have become the keystones in companies' strategic competitive policies and plans.

The development of supply chain management

Logistics beginnings

The earliest, large-scale developments in logistics probably came from military applications. Whether it was Hannibal in 218 BC crossing the Alps with 38,000 infantry, 8,000 cavalry and 37 war elephants, or the D-Day landings in 1944 when almost 3 million troops crossed the English Channel from England to Normandy, military commanders have been adept at the large-scale movement and maintenance of forces because they realized it was a battle-winning strategy. They also developed specialist organizations that could manage and implement these highly complex functions, and it is said that the foundations of modern industrial logistics were laid during World War II. Within a commercial context this type of operation was originally called the process of planning, implementing and controlling the efficient, effective flow and storage of goods, services and related information

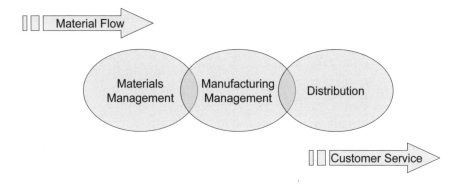

Figure 2.1 Internal logistics integration

from point of origin to point of consumption. Its aim was to deliver in such a way that it conformed to the customer's requirements – see Figure 2.1.

These definitions of a business planning and operational framework probably still sound quite logical today but it is quite noticeable that the management of relationships does not feature in them. This is because interfaces with external agencies such as upstream suppliers and downstream customers were seen as managed through formal agreements. These formal arrangements, such as contracts, ensured that the parties did not default on their obligations or 'act maliciously in their own interests'. Often considerable reliance was placed on penalty clauses to dissuade poor behaviour and performance.

Despite these contractual safeguards, it was realized that losses in value at the 'joins' between firms would inevitably lead to a reduction in internal efficiency and especially increased costs. These might include wasted time, rework or the need to hold expensive buffer stocks. Moreover, the traditional competitive strategies that emphasized the importance of employing 'economic power' as a driving objective – achieving the 'vantage point' within the supply chain – also eventually reduced value flows to supply chain members and lowered customer satisfaction. This behaviour was characterized within the UK automotive industry in the 1980s and early 1990s where head-to-head competition to obtain the lowest possible prices resulted in arm's length relationships and adversarial mistrust. It is also currently visible, to some extent, in the Australian auto business. This policy not only drove many suppliers out of business but reduced product quality to very low levels. The detrimental effect on the competitiveness of the UK automotive industry as a whole opened the door to imports from countries like Japan and South Korea, and today the UK no longer has an indigenous motor manufacturing industry, apart from niche models. It was therefore recognized that a strategy that concentrated on process efficiency alone was an inadequate response to market pressures and the stage was set for a change.

Partnership sourcing

'Partnership sourcing' was developed by pioneers such as Douglas Macbeth in the early 1990s in conjunction with the Confederation of British Industry. Rather than the usual internally focused approach, it introduced supply managers to the concept of a 'wider supply chain' that offered the potential to extend business capabilities in a rapidly globalizing, increasingly competitive environment. It primarily suggested rationalizing supplier numbers to achieve process integration and improved quality consistency through long-term relationships. However, significantly, it also emphasized the importance of a change in mindset in order to achieve the necessary commitment, trust and continuous improvement. Such purchasing partnerships were to be thought of as long-term, trusting agreements where the risks and rewards were shared.

Partnership sourcing stemmed from Japanese historical practices, including the culture of *keiretsu*. After Japan's surrender in 1945, the Allies dismantled the *zaibatsu*, the large conglomerates that dominated the country. In their place companies re-formed and re-associated into horizontally-integrated alliances across many industries; these were the original *keiretsu* companies. *Keiretsu* companies shared their suppliers, banks and other process inputs and provided mutual support to their members with a foundation in trust and a long-term perspective. The concept of *keiretsu* is graphically illustrated by Toyota's relationship policy with its suppliers, which contrasts with the traditional approach of Western automobile manufacturers. Although the assembler controls the relationship, the specialist abilities of the supplier (not present in the assembler) are recognized as being crucially important and therefore joint investments in capital, training and infrastructure are made to cement the goodwill and commitment. Partnership sourcing moved away from a traditionally adversarial view of the supply chain but it continued to accept that some companies would always dominate others, even in a paternalistic way, and that partnership remained a 'one-way street'.

Lean supply

The evolution of supply chain relationship strategies is next marked by 'lean supply'. This innovative concept transformed from a buzz-word to a major source of competitive advantage for many leading companies such as Tesco and Dell. It was developed by Dan Jones and Peter Hines in 1994 at the Lean Enterprise Research Centre in Cardiff, UK and at its core is lean thinking, which involves the understanding of waste, reducing inefficiency and finding ways to collaborate along the chain of suppliers. Each process step is broken down and fully optimized with tasks and complexity shared in order to create a frictionless flow of value-enhancing activities. The aim is to use radical techniques to do things differently, not old things better, and removing waste through lean production rather than economies of scale.

Lean supply usually requires specialized resource management skills to analyse, frame, negotiate and manage contracts and relationships. In the same way as partnership sourcing, a culture shift is essential to achieve the necessary step change, very much in the same vein is a related field known as 'agile supply chain'. Its main points, known as the seven steps, are:

1. Substitute information for inventory.

2. Work smarter not harder by eliminating or reducing non-value-adding activities.

3. Partner with suppliers to reduce in-bound lead times.

4. Seek to reduce complexity (eg, common platforms).

5. Move from push- to pull-through vendor-managed inventory.

6. Manage processes not just functions.

7. Use appropriate performance metrics (eg, time-based measures).

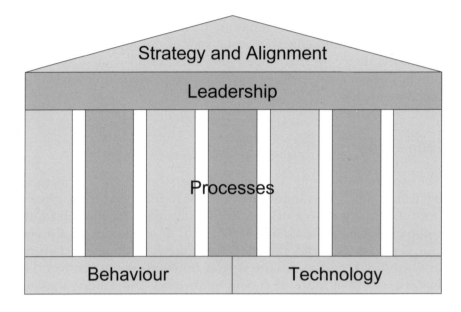

Figure 2.2 Lean supply sustainability model

More recently, lean supply has moved ahead to acknowledge the importance of sustaining the supply chain improvements achieved through process streamlining; too many supply chain initiatives have failed to meet their potential or have faded away after a year or two. Figure 2.2 illustrates the combination of factors that need to be considered to achieve and sustain process improvements.

For instance, are the strategy and organizational alignment understood, linked to reality, supported by the right KPIs, and with all departments and organizations 'on message'? Does the leadership style inspire the personnel? Have the process weak links been eradicated? Do behaviours 'live' the message and is this supported by visual management? Last, does the technology in use reinforce lean thinking and customer focus? Lean supply is a tried and tested approach that has continued to be developed since its inception. It is simple, accessible, considered to be highly effective, and has many successful supporters.

Supply chain management

SCM's roots go back to the early/mid-1990s. Its development has involved a huge number of business and academic thinkers; probably the most well-known is Richard Lamming. SCM can be viewed as an integrative, proactive approach to manage the total flow of a distribution channel to the ultimate customer, like 'a well-balanced and well-practised relay team'. Another definition of SCM that highlights its board-level importance is that it is the strategic management of the network of organizations that are involved in the upstream production and downstream distribution processes and activities associated with the satisfaction of customers, and the maximization of both current and long-term profitability. SCM is located between vertically integrated systems and those where the channel members operate completely independently. Its aims are to reduce inventory, to increase customer service reliability and build a competitive advantage for the channel. It is thus clear that relationships are of considerable importance to successful SCM.

A key feature of SCM is the early decision to reduce the number of suppliers in the chain (the elimination of multiple sourcing) because it is acknowledged that maintaining close, intense relationships can be very expensive in management effort. The intention is to have no more 'partners' than necessary and to work more closely, effectively and over the longer term, with those that have the most critical impact on the overall operation. For example, the first companies that made significant changes in this respect were Japanese lean automotive producers, such as Toyota. They typically reduced from 1,000–2,500 suppliers to about 300 suppliers. Western firms were initially slow to adopt this strategy but now this is the norm. Generally it is intended that deeper, inter-organizational alliances/partnerships will evolve and focus on the whole supply chain rather than diluting each company's efforts through conflicting goals.

Gradually, it is believed that attitudes are changing and SCM is starting to provide a business environment in which firms are able to closely cooperate rather than compete to achieve mutual goals. With fewer strategic partners working more collaboratively, there is greater incentive for joint innovation, and it is easier to share confidential demand information. This lowers uncertainty and allows a reduction in safety stocks, which then lowers costs and order cycle times. The

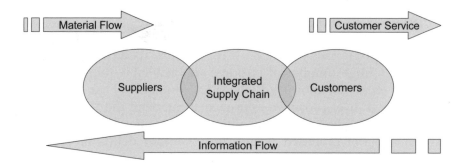

Figure 2.3 External logistics integration – SCM

relatively recent use of e-commerce is a prime example of how quality communications have facilitated these objectives. SCM's operational concepts are represented in Figure 2.3.

The integrated supply chain requires the use of new terms that hitherto had not featured in discussions about processes. Managers within these closer relationships need to consider matters such as trust, commitment, cooperation, coordination and collaboration, in addition to the more demanding choreography of complex, inter-organizational processes. It is thus generally acknowledged that SCM is not just a matter of scale but more a change of scope.

However, despite the tantalizing potential benefits of SCM, many managers wonder if it is actually possible to fully implement it. Is it a pot of gold at the end of the rainbow? Considerable progress has been made in IT to analyse and control complex processes, to fully utilize consumption data for process management, purchasing and forecasting, and to optimize whole systems of systems. But it has certainly been found that attempting to manage groups of supply chain players can be very time-consuming, wasteful of resources and more likely to drag performance backwards than promote continuous improvement. It has been suggested that achieving true supply chain integration is probably 'a lofty and difficult goal' and companies still struggle to put its principles into practice. The usual approach is to only do what is possible when convenient to do so. It is thus no wonder that, given the normal management limitations of time, budget and expertise within firms, many have been disappointed by implementations that have failed to live up to expectations. It seems that management skills must change by an order of magnitude if

SCM is to really work. This aspect is commented upon further later in the chapter.

Public sector supply chains

The review up to this point has predominantly concentrated on concepts developed in the private sector with relatively little on public sector supply chains. Most public sector organizations have adopted the latest SCM ideas and many have very modern IT and logistic facilities comparable to those used by large companies. However, the public sector is different in many ways. You only have to consider the military and its challenges of operating distribution points in remote, hostile parts of the world. Consider also the political fall-out when a soldier is killed because he was not supplied with body armour or devices on his vehicle to detect road-side bombs. Christine Harland studied aspects of the UK Health Service and listed the following distinctive features of public sector supply chains:

- *Service:* very large-scale operations dealing with highly specific services.

- *Customers:* often public sector customers are remote or widely scattered with highly specific, often time-sensitive needs, eg blood-bank users.

- *Stakeholders:* they are usually very complex, diverse and difficult to integrate and crucial to success, eg in the medical drugs arena: pharmaceutical industry bodies, government bodies, Primary Care Trusts, patients' groups, local authorities, the media.

- *Market:* the market for the supply of products used by the public sector is mostly filled with dedicated suppliers such as arms manufacturers and there are limited alternatives, eg there are few companies that manufacture MRI scanners for the health sector.

- *Accountability:* national or public interest predominates rather than shareholders. This means specific accountability is spread among a number of bodies and is often difficult to pin down precisely but nevertheless, accountability influence is just as strong.

- *Regulation:* the government makes the rules and when it is in the public interest, can 'bend' them. This may include preventing the export of sensitive technology, circumventing health and safety regulations and sanctioning monopoly.

- *Investment cycles:* public sector finance rests upon providing value for money rather than profitability. Projects thus have very long periods to generate returns on investment, eg motorway-widening projects; in defence it takes 25 years to develop a new aircraft carrier with an in-service life of 40 years or longer.

- *Government theme:* public sector supply is dependent on public spending and thus based on political decisions. Thus, if political policies change, there can be huge impacts on the way services are delivered, eg the denationalization programmes that most governments have adopted in the last 30 years.

Given the number of 'players' involved in public sector businesses it is just as important to manage relationships to deliver highly complex, often critical goods and services to very diverse customers. As SCM aims to manage a limited number of complex, business-to-business relationships over a longer term, there are thus some fundamental similarities of principle between the private and public sectors.

Small numbers

Leading on from an introduction to public sector supply chain relationships, it is clear that limited/small numbers markets will tend to exist naturally where specialized services such as utilities, health and defence are provided for the common good. 'Small numbers' are where there are reduced numbers of customers or suppliers, which produces a situation where normal competitive pressures are lowered or removed altogether. The latter position is commonly known as a monopoly. However, it is well-known that without the pressure of the market, monopolies tend to be prone to inefficiency, decay and flabbiness because costs are poorly controlled and as a result service quality is low. It is for these reasons that many of them have been deregulated in recent years and agencies such as the rail, water and phone companies have been formed to provide exposure to competitive conditions. In addition, private financing initiatives have been utilized to spread risk and tap into private sector expertise.

Nevertheless, all major governments have anti-trust laws and in the UK the work of the Competition Commission is well-publicized, for example in reviewing the trading practices of the 'big four' supermarkets. At the heart of these laws is the concept of 'public interest' but since this is usually defined by politicians rather than economists, it is open to misunderstanding and misinterpretation. It has been acknowledged that in modern markets there may be a need to collaborate in, for example, R&D and joint ventures so some reduction in competition is acceptable. Thus, despite the anti-trust activities of national governments, examples of monopolies and strong market power relationships between dominant firms in the civil sector are to be found.

Supermarket wars

Typically, the price competition 'wars' between major supermarkets with their own brands versus global companies such as Marlboro cigarettes, Coca-Cola and Pepsi, and between major market players such as Wal-Mart and Rubbermaid, in the early/mid-1990s, displayed some archetypal characteristics of monopolistic 'bad behaviour'.

The giant brand owners initially forced the supermarkets to support high prices for their products. In response, the latter promoted the development of high quality alternatives such as Virgin Cola and Cott Corporation carbonated drink products. This eventually restored the balance of power and prevented destructive, adversarial influences from destroying long-term, profitable relationships. Although Wal-Mart was able to force Rubbermaid to climb down over price level maintenance, without the support of the Wal-Mart market, Rubbermaid subsequently lost its direction and market share. Eventually Wal-Mart stepped in to prevent Rubbermaid from failing.

Limited markets are not areas that generally command a great deal of attention. Nevertheless, consider a collaborative relationship that your company has developed with another. Substantial time and effort will have been expended exploring and defining the business proposition. Infrastructure and systems have been modified at great expense, precious intellectual property has been shared, staff have been trained and possibly seconded to the partner firm, and valuable market knowledge has been contributed. The overall aim has been compelling: to bring to bear a unique bundle of resources and capabilities to produce a seamless, cost-efficient channel to market that will beat the competition. But a key success factor, inter-dependence, has actually created a bilateral monopoly situation where, although both partners are free to leave if they wish, the cost and disruption of this action could be almost unthinkable. Interdependence involves mutual agreement to share the work and thus depend upon the other partner. Any loss in autonomy is compensated through the expected gains. As long as the relationship is well-managed and fresh, the need to 'divorce' does not arise but, if complacency sets in and is left unchecked, the door is opened to inefficiency, decay and flabbiness. There is an obvious correlation here between the sort of situation found in a monopoly and that in a truly collaborative relationship. The 'locked-in' factor is therefore a further challenge to the successful operation of partnered business relationships.

Supply chain networks

Supply chains have been described as linear, upstream purchasing and downstream selling relationships to which SCM has added shared responsibility for the health and performance of the overall chain relationship. However, practical supply chain relationships are rarely linear. When viewed from the perspective of the manufacturer, industrial networks consist of pairs of firms in close relationships forming focal, value-added partnerships. Together with a secondary network of other firms they manage the flow of goods and services around a specific market opportunity. Networks can also be viewed as hub-and-spoke structures with a leading organization at the 'hub' organizing the exchanges between the other firms. Each participating firm is able to concentrate on its area of special competence and leave other activities to the other network members. The conditions that give rise to networks are commonly where very complex tasks need to be performed under pressure of time or finance, where specialized knowledge is compartmentalized amongst firms, or where a group of organizations need to defend themselves against a strong competitor. Sometimes they originate from trade associations, but they are most common in high-technology industries such as computers, semi-conductors, aircraft manufacturing and biotechnology. The Toyota motor company is an example of a modern networking hub organization. One hundred and eighty primary or first-tier firms supply component parts and undertake research with Toyota, which allows it the 'freedom' to concentrate on the design and manufacture of automobiles.

The difficulty of managing supply chain partnering arrangements has already been mentioned; in network situations the complexities are an order of magnitude greater. There are four important integrating factors within supply chain networks: equipment and resources, human resources, material and inventory, and facility configuration. The critical success factors are risk and benefit sharing, conflict resolution and information sharing. The challenge for managers is to balance the individual goals of the firm with those of the group; however, contracts are not straightforward or easy to enforce. It is more difficult to maintain focus on objectives when the member firms have different reasons for joining the consortium. There is greater scope for communication problems and misunderstanding. Coordination will be harder to achieve and power and politics will look for opportunities to take an unfair advantage.

Some networks have been defined as 'constellations of businesses' that organize through the establishment of social rather than legally binding contracts. As a result of dealing closely with partners over time, firms reduce environmental uncertainty, they manage their dependence on each other, they gain cost efficiency and achieve satisfaction and kudos from working within a peer group. However, these situations are not any easier to manage than more traditional structures. Experience seems to show that rather than managing proactively, networked firms have difficulty in following any particular management strategy. They prefer instead to 'drift' with the group and cope with change by being reactive.

Strategic alliances

Strategic alliances should not be confused with joint ventures. If the end point of partnering can be considered as vertical integration in the form of acquisition, then the step immediately prior to that can be thought of as a joint venture. Typically in a joint venture a separate organization is set up. This organization can be staffed wholly or in part with employees of the sponsoring organizations, but generally its distinguishing characteristic is the presence of joint ownership by the sponsors. This can be in the form of common shareholding, leasing of site or other capital, all backed by copious legal and contractual obligations. Joint ventures are traditionally formed to exploit an opportunity slightly peripheral to the firm's strategic focus. Their scope is more conservative and involves less risk with more definitive investments and objectives.

Definitions of strategic alliances abound, but the general consensus is that they have strategic rather than tactical significance, and have a longer-term outlook than other partnerships. Strategic alliances do not involve the creation of a new business entity. The firms involved support the arrangement with a range of specialized inputs such as know-how and manpower (although some investment in equity is not without precedent) just as they would for normal partnerships. However, the ambition of a strategic alliance is typically of critical importance to the firms concerned and often involves significant risk because of the resources they bring together and the external forces that they push against.

Historically, alliances have been bi-polar; that is, two firms would form a strategic alliance. However, while this remains the most common form, they are becoming increasingly multi-faceted with, for instance, alliance-based networks consisting of firms that combine with several other non-competitive firms in a consortium to achieve a common objective.

The Boston Consulting Group describes four types of alliance:

1. *Expertise alliances* – where firms share expertise and capabilities such as in the licensing of new drug compounds in bio-pharmaceuticals.

2. *New business alliances* – partnerships where non-competing firms look to exploit a new business or market.

3. *Cooperative alliances* – such as purchasing groups, trade and industry associations or political lobby groups where competitors combine to achieve critical mass.

4. *Merger and acquisition* – where the alliance is a substitute for a merger that is inhibited by legal or commercial factors.

The two most common types are technological and marketing alliances. Technological alliances involve cooperation in activities such as R&D, engineering, information systems and manufacturing. They pool the intellectual prowess of two or more firms and can engage in cost and risk sharing, product development, learning, and achieving increased speed to market. R&D alliances often bring together small firms with specific technical skills and larger firms with experience in development and manufacturing. By pooling their complementary skills these firms can typically produce a product faster and cheaper than individual firms could alone. Marketing alliances typically match a company with a distribution system that is attractive to another that is trying to increase the sales of a product or service. For example, a US food company may form an alliance with Nestlé to gain access to its distribution channels in Europe. The strategic logic of this type of alliance for both partners is simple: by finding more outlets for its products, the supplying partner can increase economies of scale and reduce unit costs. The partner that provides the distribution channel benefits by adding products to its portfolio. Studies have examined the benefits of both technological and marketing alliances and found in the pharmaceutical industry that a firm's rate of new product development is a function of the number of strategic alliances that it has entered. In new, high-technology ventures there was a positive linkage between sales growth and the use of R&D collaborative arrangements.

Alliances rarely have simple, single defined objectives. At best they enable firms to collaboratively exploit the competences and resources that they bring together as a team. In consequence, they increasingly focus on complex systems and solutions that require multiple skill sets and innovation. In contrast to other forms of partnering, the relationships between the parties involved can be ambiguous. Whereas it is possible to talk about the 'channel captain' in marketing channels, or identify the roles performed by the various actors in a supply chain or supplier/customer partnership, the relationships between members of an R&D alliance can be less hierarchical or departmentalized. It is partially as a consequence of this free-form nature that alliances are notoriously difficult to manage and yet often produce the most compelling and constructive benefits for firms to establish a relationship.

Marketing channels

Marketing channels contain sets of interdependent, intermediary organizations involved in the process of making a product or service available for use or consumption. They thus bridge the gap between the manufacturing facility and the final consumer. Intermediaries ensure that products and services are available to end-users when and where required. In reality this involves a sophisticated structure of collaborative relationships and it is for this reason that their operation, strategic significance and management issues are described next.

Philip Kotler, the marketing guru, was clear that a firm's decision to employ indirect channels and a customer's requirement to buy through intermediaries largely boils down to their superior efficiency in making goods widely available and accessible to target markets. This superior efficiency creates its own value that would not exist if the manufacturer did not collaborate with the reseller and if the manufacturer was not inclined to invest in the human resources of the intermediary through training, certification and incentive programmes.

Manufacturers, distributors and retailers have all recognized that the management of distribution channel activities provides significant opportunities for firms to create strategic advantage and achieve extraordinary financial performance. Channel activities are thus a major source of value-added benefits for end-users, arguably even greater than the value added by other marketing activities. Specifically, it is the manner in which marketing channels complement or round-off the product offering of the manufacturing firm to the end-customers that makes the difference. It is this difference that an individual firm would find difficult to copy. In the battle to provide end-customers with superior value, manufacturing firms are recognizing that the benefits of marketing channels lie not only in their potential for greater efficiencies or their ability to add value but in their unique abilities to provide customers with a 'transaction experience' that addresses their diverse and broad needs and requirements. Martin Christopher of Cranfield School of Management describes this combination of physical and intangible components that comprise a marketing channel as 'marketing logistics'.

Essential intermediaries

Channel marketing intermediaries perform a number of different functions; two of the most important are the fulfilment and stimulation of customer demand. Intermediaries can often provide these services and functions more efficiently or effectively than the manufacturer. Many firms tend to focus only on the first and as a result intermediaries are often seen as a necessary (and unwelcome) link between the firm and its customers. They are distrusted because it is believed they only respond to customer demand and are thus likely to be disloyal and liable to switch brands and take short-term advantage whenever possible. In effect they are viewed as parasitic to the vendor's efforts in stimulating demand and brand loyalty. Alternatively, they are seen as 'mere' logistical operations; a simple outsourcing decision made by the firm's distribution and warehouse organization. Although these views are not generally voiced openly, they often lie beneath the surface of many management discussions and will forestall flexibility and reinforce limiting controls. Such a position is usually based on ignorance of marketing logistics or perhaps a single bad experience that becomes generalized. The consequence is clear: treating channels in this way will negate any benefits that the channel could offer. It will also bring about more opportunistic behaviour as the channel reciprocates and amplifies the level of mistrust.

Channels bring the output from a range of manufacturers into an environment where the consumer can browse, access and evaluate before purchase. Also, few products or services are purchased or consumed in isolation from other products. The resellers therefore extend their product portfolio to include associated products. For example, a sports equipment store will sell tennis racquets and tennis balls; a PC reseller will sell PCs and printers; and a boutique will sell shirts and ties. In these ways intermediaries can balance the assortment between various manufacturers' portfolios and the needs of the consumer in terms of quality, range and associated products.

Resellers can also influence the level of demand in the market. Stimulating customer demand by resellers has two dimensions – first, resellers will generate demand for product classes and categories, such as more tennis racquets or more football shoes in a sports outfitters; secondly, they can be incentivized and motivated to stimulate demand for a specific brand and model. These services relieve the manufacturer of a complex task that depends on local market knowledge and which, if done well by the intermediary, provide all channel players with additional revenues.

To achieve cost advantages or competitive parity manufacturers prefer transactions to be in economic quantities. The wholesalers and distributors take bulk quantities into storage and reduce them into individually saleable units. Increasingly some manufacturers are employing advanced processes to enable them to customize individual units to meet the specific requests of customers directly. This might be customizing cars to specific customer requirements, eg colour and interior specification, or building a PC with the required software pre-loaded. But it is usually at the channel-consumer interface that these customizations are brought to reality.

Intermediaries also ensure that there is a commonality and consistency in the way that the actual purchase transaction takes place, irrespective of the geographic location of the manufacturer, its organizational type (non-profit versus profit making, independent company or government agency), and its objectives. Intermediaries ensure that all transactions are standardized so that the customer does not have to consider any variation between the terms and conditions of buying one brand or another.

As a process, therefore, channels can be seen as taking input from manufacturers either directly from production or from stock, holding it in stock or supplying back to back against customer demand. The functions that they perform are against time, location, allocation, assortment, searching and routinalization. These functions are described as the marketing channel primary service outputs, shown in Figure 2.4, but they are essentially dependent for their success on the channel end-to-end relationships.

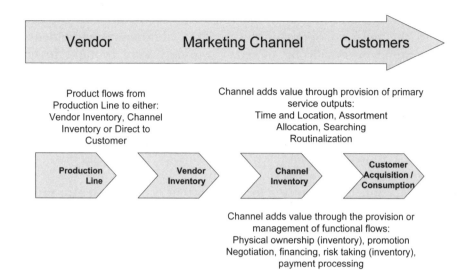

Figure 2.4 Marketing channel primary service outputs

The channel also takes on board the management of functional flows such as moving inventory or finance. In many instances the provision of these functions is separate from their management, for example the intermediary can manage the payment process on behalf of a banking organization (which may or may not be the actual manufacturer of the goods).

Channel dynamism

Marketing channel complexity is nowadays associated with speed of change resulting from shifting bases of power and the emergence of new routes to market. All of these increase the challenge in providing even greater choice for the consumer. Channel success is thus dependent on the ability of managers to adapt quickly and efficiently.

In the past, channels have been considered as static with a built in inertia to change that was rooted in their very complexity and the established pattern of doing business between independent firms. Personal relationships established over a long time meant that it was difficult to change existing channel partners. Bringing on new partners needed a round of meetings and negotiations to explore both the business opportunities and the contractual agreements that would eventually be signed. Customers were thought to be traditional in their purchasing habits, and reluctant to buy products from anywhere other than trusted and tried outlets.

All this has changed and today even the most established and traditional distribution channels are increasingly subject to change, if not at a revolutionary pace, then at least much more rapidly than before. Within some channels such as high-tech, fashion and financial services, the changes are very swift. This accelerated change has been made possible by advances in technology that make it easier for firms to manage complex systems. IT can provide the data to evaluate the sales performance of channels, provide information, and facilitate communication as well as manage the necessary logistics and finance operations.

The strategic importance of marketing channels

It is clear that marketing channels broaden the scope of many intermediary-manufacturer relationships which, if not actually strategic, are formed with a common and agreed purpose. It is also very clear that the success of marketing channels is dependent on the sum of their parts, ie the success of each firm depends on all the others coordinating their efforts towards the single objective of satisfying customers.

Failing to appreciate the role of the channel can cost you your job; at least that was the experience of Michael Capellas, the former chief at Compaq who was ousted in November 2002 following the firm's merger with Hewlett-Packard. One reason for his departure quoted by the press was his lack of commitment and understanding of channels; this demonstrates the importance being placed on marketing channels by major corporations. Even those whose heritage and previous success rested on large direct sales organizations are increasingly adopting indirect channels, either to replace or to complement their established direct sales forces. This shift in strategic emphasis reflects the realization that indirect channels can, in many instances, do things better, quicker and cheaper than the manufacturing firm. Moreover, they are viewed by boards as a key component in the creation of economic value and competitive advantage. However, such benefits do not come without increased complexity. The management of channels, their processes and their relationships, is very challenging, especially when the concept of channel relationship management is not understood or practised.

Managing buy-sell relationships

Many organizations have embraced the ideas of supply chain and marketing channel relationships as ways of extending their search for lower costs and improved products and services. They have created a range of partnerships that now represent significant, often strategic assets in their business configuration. Later in this book we will describe a number of ways that managers can tackle the task of getting the best possible performance from their relationships. But at this point, the review of the development of partnerships would not be complete without considering the specific seller and buyer perspectives, because in the end they will have to be reconciled and managed.

The seller perspective

Organization changes have forced firms to move away from strait-jacketed cultures that were characterized by their overt sales orientation and win-lose mentality. Management initiatives such as quality management, reengineering and lean six sigma have continued to attack sales process costs. While driving for ever lower levels of sales, administration and general costs (SAG), firms are being forced to seek the benefits only available to effective partnering and outsourcing. Accordingly, the business schools and gurus have urged sales managers to take a more analytical and structured approach to dealing with their important customers. Given that business-to-business relationships may take many forms, and firms may be involved in more than one at any time, managers should classify their customers according to their importance and adopt a portfolio approach to create and manage appropriate relationships, as illustrated in Figure 2.5.

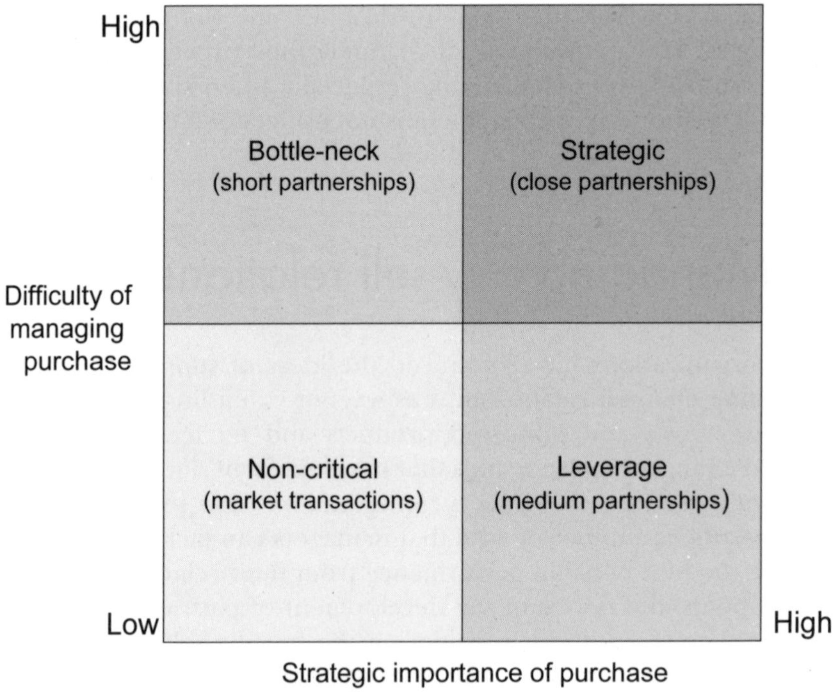

Figure 2.5 Portfolio management model

This idea evolved into 'New marketing', which proposed that all marketing activities should be directed towards establishing, developing and maintaining successful relationships. It involves 'designing and negotiating strategic partnerships with vendors and technology partners through whom the firm deploys its distinctive competences to serve market opportunities'. Thus, relationships rather than sales became the prime focus. The key technique that emerged from new marketing was key account management (KAM). Malcolm McDonald proposed that the strategic importance of relationship-building and maintenance to the long-term profitability of a supplier needed to be recognized by the appointment of senior managers to provide the necessary high level expertise and pan-firm perspective. KAM has been implemented successfully by a wide variety of organizations such as American Express and Citibank.

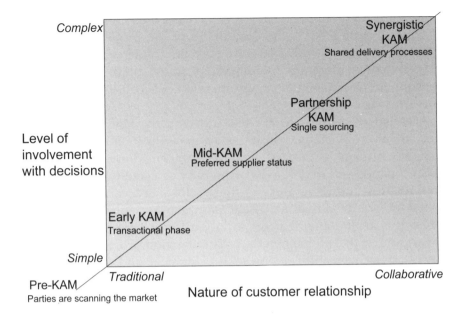

Figure 2.6 Key account relationship development model

The KAM concept has become very well known through the work of Malcolm McDonald and is used to describe the spectrum of relationship types shown in Figure 2.6. It can also be viewed as a development path as relationships mature either up or down the slope, and firms may form relationships that enter and leave the graph at any level.

Pre-KAM indicates the parties are scanning the market; early KAM is a transactional stage; mid-KAM suggests a preferred supplier; partnership KAM is single sourcing, and synergistic KAM refers to shared process delivery. KAM relationships are therefore important and complex, often involving the customization of products and services as well as pricing and distribution functions in the interests of developing longer-term, collaborative relationships. Such relationships yield the supplier higher revenues and faster growth rates, while customers benefit from having their objectives met and enjoying faster response times.

In many instances within supply chains, the adoption of KAM practices by suppliers is driven by the demands of customers as they rationalize their supplier base and increase their demands on the remaining suppliers. As the capabilities of the preferred suppliers develop, the incentive for customers to build longer-term relationships with them increases. As this is reciprocated, there is an incentive for suppliers to manage their customers as key accounts and to create true win–win situations.

Although KAM has clearly demonstrated the ability to increase the effectiveness of relationship management, its implementation in many firms is haphazard. The decision on where to locate the KAM function – as part of a department or as a standalone group, at business unit or directorate level, and at global or local level – is often taken for irrational reasons. The KAM function achieves best results when it is an independent organization located under a powerful directorate with a global mandate. This location provides it with the necessary strategic information such as financial and sales models to allow it to fully understand the 'costs to serve' and thus effectively manage customer profitability. It will also be the influence within the company that ensures consistency of service and prices across sales boundaries.

The role of the KAM department is often misunderstood by organizations. Rather than overseeing the portfolio of strategically important customers to generate long-term returns, a number of firms continue to impose short-term sales targets on their KAMs. These have the effect of 'pushing' inappropriate products or quantities and subverting the strategic relationships and their long-term revenue plans.

The buyer perspective

Collaborative relationships between customers and suppliers have become the new hot topic in strategic procurement. However, there is a real danger that buyers may not be getting the most out of their collaborative relationships because they are still using traditional management and measurement approaches that are not sufficiently systematic or integrated. 'Collaboration' really does mean sharing: not just the operational management of the relationship, but also the skills and experience that generate valuable learning opportunities. This means that unlocking the value potential in a collaborative relationship requires new ways of measuring relationship quality that go beyond the normal financial and operational KPIs. Customers that still treat their key suppliers as 'junior partners' in a collaborative relationship, and continue to measure relationship quality using traditional supplier performance measures, may be missing out on many of the potential benefits.

In many organizations the matter of professional relationship management is often left entirely to chance. Traditionally the task has been 'picked up' by the responsible sales person who wishes to keep the customer happy post-sale and has his or her eye on the next one. The sales person has no official responsibility over other parts of the company such as design and operations that will contribute to delivering the outputs, and he or she will often be viewed by them as someone who interferes with their work. Procurement managers face a number of further difficulties. Despite the presence of good contracts, operational failures and poor teamwork will often lead organizations to a focus on the 'small print' and selfish behaviours rather than patiently building long-term value for the customer. A traditional emphasis on the management of time, cost and quality, often called supplier or project management, usually ignores the importance of teamwork between customer and suppliers and pays little attention to the underlying causes of difficulty. These often occur 'below the radar level' and by the time they emerge may seriously damage the relationship. In addition to this, the supplier organizations may well be operating a KAM system. Although this aims to maintain strategic relationships for the longer term, its approach focuses on its own 'revenue stream maximization', which is essentially supplier-centric. There is thus a clash of management attitudes and cultures. Procurement managers are likely to see the warning signs and might know what is happening, but they don't know why. Examples of these are:

- complacency (accepting average performance and normalization of problems);
- distrust (failures to perform cause self-centred behaviours);
- opportunism (seeking gain at the expense of the partnership);
- quality failures (unresolved joint process problems);
- poor communication ('fuzzy' channels);

- cost overruns (internal optimization resulting in increased joint costs);

- late deliveries (process hiccups multiply at organization interfaces).

The common result is much management time spent fire-fighting symptoms rather than tackling root causes, and sometimes in frustration, invoking penalty clauses with the inevitable dangers of diminishing joint performance and relationship fracture.

The joint perspective

A number of major organizations such as Hewlett-Packard, Xerox and Coca-Cola have come to the conclusion that they need to consolidate their procurement activities into a single focus with the ability and status to maximize value creation from collaboration with customers and suppliers. They have put in place a dedicated alliance management function charged with 'institutionalizing' collaborative processes and systems and spreading know-how throughout the company. The function also coordinates relationship activity across departments and ensures the necessary resources are provided to support the alliance activities. Importantly, this initiative has also stimulated the creation and use of alliance metrics that allow alliance managers to systematically evaluate performance. As a result, companies like these have a 25 per cent higher alliance success rate and generated almost four times the market wealth compared to others.

The alliance function will not work effectively if it is a secondary commercial or sales one, nor should it be diffused across departments. It is essential that it has a strategic and central focus, preferably close to board level. Critically, without objective performance measurement providing the right knowledge to monitor, steer and improve activities, the relationship value achieved will be below its potential.

A number of best practice 'tips' have emanated from strategic procurement thinking:

- Centralize the management of your key supplier relationships in a single, professional team.

- Recognize that relationship managers are experienced, knowledgeable, high-integrity people; recruit, train and reward them accordingly.

- Keep relationship managers in post for reasonable periods – don't rotate them onto another project just as they are building the trust-based supplier links that are vital if full value is to be captured.

- Task relationship managers with aligning the parent company functions that service its relationships.

- Encourage collaborative planning and forecasting with key suppliers.

- Engage in 'adult-to-adult' conversations with suppliers; recognize that they are experts in what they do, and may be able to solve your problems for you.

- Introduce appropriate metrics to measure and monitor relationship performance.

- Reward problem-solving and creative behaviours.

- Involve other supply chain partners.

Conclusion

This chapter has traced the development of relational business dealings in the supply chain in both private and public sector guises. It has described the complexity of partnering within marketing channels and considered the management of business relationships from seller and buyer perspectives. The need for process improvement within supply chains has been shown to have reached its limit along with how companies have sought to achieve lasting competitive market positions through closer, more collaborative relationships with a partner or networks of partners.

Relational associations based on cooperative operations now represent strategic assets to many firms. Furthermore, new attitudes and specialized management techniques are essential to reap the benefits. The next chapter highlights the key factors that inhibit or hinder, and those that promote or drive successful relationships.

Key action points

1. Categorize your important commercial relationships according to their type: linear supply chain, supply chain network, strategic alliance, marketing channel and buy-sell.

2. How effective do you think is the level of teamwork that you have in this relationship(s)?

3. What type of management do you use for these relationships? Is it KAM, supplier management or joint (relationship management)?

4. Why have you adopted this approach? Is it for historical reasons, because you always have used this approach?

5. What is the effectiveness of this management approach?

3 The obstacles and drivers of successful partnerships

If we are together nothing is impossible. If we are divided all will fail.

(Winston Churchill)

Introduction

It is recognized that not all partnerships live up to the expectations placed upon them. However, lessons can be learnt that increase the likelihood of a successful, collaborative partnership. The gains from these successful relationships can translate into substantial competitive advantages for the firm involved and secure long-term, superior returns. The competences and knowledge required and acquired for successfully managing a partnership are transferable skills. Companies that are successful in managing one relationship are likely to be successful in managing others. Sadly the converse is also true. We have seen firms repeat the same mistakes in many different relationships and then blame the various partners for the failure rather than looking at the common denominator.

This chapter looks at some of the important drivers and obstacles to successful relationships and how an understanding of these factors can impact the business performance. Traditionally there are three factors seen as critical to successful partnerships: the ability to leverage assets, the ability to learn from and exploit the knowledge gleaned from a partnership and, crucially, the skills and competence in managing the partnership and its resources. It is argued that there is a fourth element that is typically missing in many partnerships, namely measurement. Firms will measure inputs and outputs but rarely give thought to the partnering process itself. It is clear that effective partnering measurement is the hallmark of many successful relationships, and this chapter outlines the challenges of practically measuring this performance and acting on the information pro-actively.

Leveraging mutual investments

If we were doing this ourselves, we would spend at least three times as much, and run a high risk.

(Chia Song Hwee, Chief Executive, Chartered Semiconductor, on its partnership with IBM and Samsung)

The benefits that firms can gain from their partnerships are a direct result of the time, effort and physical resources they invested in the relationship. These investments can take various forms such as a particular facility, IT system, or market knowledge. They are solely applicable and relevant to the partnership itself and are unlikely to have any value or at least a greatly reduced value outside of the relationship. For example, the co-location of warehousing facilities by a supplier with its manufacturer customer can reduce supply chain costs such as transport. It can also improve supply chain efficiency through greater flexibility, by ensuring timely delivery and by creating opportunities for immediate problem resolution and process refinement.

Dell Inc provides a good example of using co-location of warehousing. Many of Dell's suppliers are located in South East Asia with consequential long lead times on delivery. To create a buffer against demand, suppliers hold inventory local to the Austin, Texas assembly facility in 'revolver carousel racks' (known as 'revolving' inventory). These supplier logistics centres (SLCs) are small warehouses shared between a number of suppliers that are located within a few miles of Dell's assembly plants. Crucially, Dell does not own the inventory but the cost of maintaining inventory in the supply chain is, by necessity, passed on by the suppliers and included in the final prices of the computers. This not only improves Dell's balance sheet, but also ensures that the inventory levels are managed closest to the factory line.

The partnership investments need not be capital or physical assets. Human assets can also be important, for example in the establishment and training of dedicated sales personnel. Even less tangible assets like process competence and knowledge bases can be investments that can be leveraged.

But many firms simply fail to invest in their relationships or partnerships. The idea of relying on third parties causes many firms to become even more risk averse and less keen to invest, especially in capital projects. Moreover, a firm's reluctance to invest sends a signal to the partnership (and often to the market as well) that it lacks commitment. The result is that development is slowed, profits are not generated at the expected rate, market benefits may be lost and a potentially successful alliance may fail.

Where the partners have built up a level of trust, there is likely to be less 'holding back'. This reduces fears of uncertainty and firms are more likely to be confident in making investments. For example, by establishing a service desk on the premises of a major customer to handle queries and problems on the spot, the supplier is demonstrating commitment, ensuring that issues cannot escalate and generating loyalty. This kind of investment is also likely to build trust even further and increase the chance of cooperation and invest-ment being reciprocated.

The investment case is not easy to write, however, because it must be framed in the light of the expectation that the partnership will last, is worth investing in, and that trust and commitment are present or potentially present on both sides. The initiative for the investment should have at its heart an appreciation of its value in the partnership. Firms can sometimes make investments that are purely in their own self-interest and then bemoan the fact that the partner does not make use of them. The business case would also have to include a comparison between the level of investment a firm would need to make if it wanted to achieve the same end goals but had chosen to act independently. This is consistent with in-house versus outsourcing arguments, but can be applied to inward investment in a partnership and requires a degree of informed guesswork as well as due diligence research. The in-house/outsourcing evaluation can be extended beyond traditional financial boundaries to consider the value that is created as a consequence of the partnership or alliance. The value generated through such investments is not singular and may be seen by the end-customer differently to the original manufacturer. This is demonstrated in the case of Novell's accreditation and certification programmes, which created significant value for end-customers in the form of advice, support and reliability. It also created value for Novell's partners in the form of incremental revenue streams. For Novell itself, the value was captured in the form of loyal resellers, retained customers and a growing reputation and market share. Firms can make a fundamental error and value the benefit of an investment solely from their perspective while a shift in focus and evaluation to the partner's point of view may be enlightening.

The partnership investment can become complicated when the assets become 'stranded'. Stranded assets are investments that no longer represent value to the partnership, or have not been utilized, or have been leveraged differently than originally envisaged. They may be considered as being unsympathetic to the aims of the part-nership or interpreted by the prospective recipients as contrary to their own commercial interests. For example, an investment on the part of a manufacturer in demonstration facilities for its partners may not be used for a number of reasons.

Partners may be sceptical about the aims of the investment and whether the host firm will use it to take unfair advantage, eg directly approach customers brought into the showroom. Assets can be stranded when the surrounding and supporting processes are not partner-friendly and are often extensions of internal procedures and formats, ie booking time slots and facilities at the showroom requires multiple sign-offs and approvals.

Firms may invest in its partnership and simply fail to communicate its availability to the partners; this is not uncommon in broader partnership structures such as marketing channels. In some instances these investments may be considered to be nothing more than poor or misjudged management decisions, eg the partners already have their own demonstration facilities in-house. In partnering contracts, stranded assets can become the grounds for recriminations, ie, 'We gave them what they asked for, and now they don't use it!' We have investigated instances of such non-usage of programmes and initiatives that have caused friction and resentment by the host. Typically this non-usage can be attributed to poor communication, mismatch of expectations and requirements, and process delivery inefficiencies.

Novell: a lesson in channel marketing

In the 1980s and 1990s Novell was a small Utah-based company that was facing the might of IBM and Digital with their hordes of end-user sales people, and continuing pressure coming from Microsoft. Its networking software, Netware, offered advanced features and functionality that allowed users to connect together PCs, Apple Macs and even link into mainframes. But its complexity also meant that it was not easy to install and some could argue it was prone to 'falling over'. Novell's home ground was the small and medium-sized business market (SMB). Competing against IBM and Digital in the corporate space was always going to be its biggest challenge, and with an average network of less than 10 clients (even though at the far end Netware was being used to connect hundreds and thousands of PCs), Novell targeted the mass SMB market.

Novell's solution was to engage with the PC partners and offer them a product that helped them to add value to their services. Of equal significance, the technical expertise needed was 'productized' such that partners could become accredited to resell and install Netware, giving them a competitive edge. Netware accreditation was cleverly devised. Partners' accreditation came as a consequence of having the right number of staff trained as Certified Netware Engineers (CNEs). To enable this and Novell established specialized Novell Authorized Training Centres that were profit contributors in themselves. CNEs became increasingly in demand, moving from one partner to another and seeing their income grow as a result. To become a CNE was not easy; it involved a number of courses that took time and money. Once trained, CNEs had to make sure that they kept up to date with new products and revisions.

Having a CNE was only the start of the process. Novell's Platinum partners, the top end of the scale, had to make even greater investments in people and equipment. In return, partners received support from Novell that was second to none, almost instantaneous access to Novell's technical labs, and sales leads and marketing support. The channel was run virtually as a franchise operation and while Novell continued to respond with world-class products that offered highly lucrative service and annuity margins, the channel remained happy and loyal. The success of Novell was such that in 1991, IBM dropped Microsoft's LAN Manager networking solution and adopted Netware as part of its product offering.

The investment that Novell made in its channel partners was substantial. This was reciprocated by the investment levels that Novell's partners made to maintain their level of accreditation. Both parties fully leveraged these investments to the benefit of their businesses and customers.

Learning from each other

An organization's ability to learn, and translate that learning into action rapidly, is the ultimate competitive advantage.

(Jack Welch, CEO of General Electric)

It cannot be assumed that the gains from asset leverage will simply materialize. Of critical importance to the creation of competitive advantage is inter-organizational learning that comes about as a result of collaboration. This competitive advantage can occur through creating the climate and conditions for substantial knowledge exchange. This then leads to joint learning and, through the heightened ability to leverage the relationship investments, the creation of new products, services and technologies. Thus, establishing a regular pattern of inter-firm interactions that support the transfer, recombination or creation of specialized knowledge is likely to bring considerable benefits to both partners. Many IT manufacturers will provide full or partial funding for a dedicated person within a reseller partner, recognizing the sales productivity gains to be achieved by establishing experience in performing specific tasks and creating an investment that can be leveraged. These individuals also enable the transfer of factual knowledge on product functionality to the partner and ensure that less tangible knowledge about 'how the business is done' flows between intermediary and manufacturer. This simultaneously encourages better information flow and service delivery to the end-customer.

A firm's ability to recognize and digest valuable information from a particular alliance partner is a function of: a) establishing frequent opportunities to exchange key information (eg, planning, design, marketing and other meetings) and to support this with social interactions that help people to get to know each other; and b) the extent to which partners have overlapping knowledge bases (you can't assimilate if you don't understand).

The Michelin tyre company provides its specialist users, such as earth moving and military vehicle operators, with free training and regular product maintenance update briefings. These occasions allow the company to get useful feedback on how its products are used, comments on design, and ideas for product improvements and the effectiveness of its maintenance procedures. Thus, firms need to ensure that the appropriate processes and resources are in place for the collection and sharing of tangible data and processes. It also means that firms must be able to assimilate intangible know-how and experience, which is much more culturally and organizationally driven. Many partnerships focus on the first aspect of information-sharing without considering the second. The ability to exploit out-side sources of knowledge is largely a function of experience and being able to recognize the value of new information and then being able to derive commercial benefit from it. This shows why firms from dissimilar markets and industries often struggle to come together successfully: a lack of common language, common experience and reference points hinders knowledge transfer and thus the likelihood of collaborative success.

Firms that wish to gain from their partnerships and alliances therefore need to ensure that both culturally and structurally they create the environment in which inter-organizational learning can flourish. In this sense 'culture' may or may not be to do with the particular part of the world they are from but more about firms coming together with a common view of business and the desire to learn from each other. Such cultural differences were apparent in the Hewlett-Packard/Microsoft alliance in which HP hosted MS Exchange on its servers. The alliance almost floundered due to a clash of culture and leadership styles. The solution was found in recognizing the different approaches and finding ways to leverage and assimilate the alternative ways of working.

While the gains from inter-organizational learning can be substan-tial, few firms seem to get as much from these relationships as they wished or as potentially available. Traditionally, some firms have been averse to seeking new skills and competences from their partners because they believe it would suggest a weakness or failing that the other firm would look to exploit. Trends are now emerging that indicate that firms are less reticent about their sourcing of know-how and understanding from partners. In many leading firms, partners are now an equal source of ideas alongside employees and ahead of traditional sources such as trade associations and even academia, to the extent that creative innovation is firmly established on a foundation of inter-organizational learning and cultural openness.

Automotive symbiotic relationships

Consider the case of US and Japanese car manufacturing during the second half of the 20th century. From today's perspective, it seems strange to consider that at one point the Japanese motor industry was concerned about the impact of globalization on their market and the force of the US automobile giants.

Just after the end of World War II, firms like Toyota recognized the need to improve on their reputation for low quality production while achieving the same levels of cost-efficiencies as their US rivals. Moreover, they had to achieve this within the confines of a limited market with lower levels of capital and investment. The next 30 to 40 years mirror the development of the total quality management (TQM) methodologies as the resultant continuous improvement enabled the Japanese firms to turn the tables and grow into powerful competitors to the US firms, utilizing their lean and agile production capabilities and competencies. Lower costs were matched by improved and world-renowned quality and innovation. In response to serious commercial and financial woes in their domestic market, Ford, Chrysler and General Motors all sought alliances with Japanese firms in an attempt to stave off the inroads they were making into the US domestic market. Ford was the first to move by taking a minority stake-holding in Toyo Kogyo whose brands included Mazda and more recently Xedos. Toyo Kogyo's capabilities were ahead of its own local competitors despite its then financially challenged situation. Toyo Kogyo was not only enjoying low manufacturing costs, but more significantly, its costs were falling at a faster rate than its rivals. Between its sites in Hiroshima and Hama, Toyo Kogyo offered Ford access to the most flexible and focused automotive manufacturing sites in Japan and unparalleled opportunities to acquire new skills and process knowledge.

Toyota formulated a strategic alliance with General Motors in 1984, which had been forced to lay off staff at a number of its facilities in the wake of falling market share and profitability. The NUMMI project called for the two firms to manufacture compact cars at a GM site in California. Japanese and US managers would work side by side, which allowed General Motors to learn lean production methodologies alongside a master, while at the same time testing and trialling them with a US workforce. Chrysler was not to be left out. Its alliance with Mitsubishi allowed it to source product and components more effectively, survive financial difficulties and learn new techniques. By the 1990s Chrysler was reputably the most competent product developer in the US auto industry.

The benefits were not simply one-sided. The Japanese firms won the propaganda war. Collaboration alongside the US workforce earned them major kudos with the domestic public. In fact, the success of the various initiatives suggested that it wasn't the US blue-collar worker who was deficient, but the US management that was at fault, alleviating the blame that had originally been cast at Japan for the loss of jobs in the domestic motor industry. Toyota learnt about US labour practices and Toyo Kogyo learnt how to design for the US driver. But perhaps the most important lesson that the Japanese firms learnt was how to sell to the US consumer and how to compete as an equal in the US market. These were lessons that Japanese companies would apply in earnest over the coming decade.

Governance

So far we have shown that a firm's ability to enjoy 'relational rents' – that is, supernormal profits, jointly generated in a partnering relationship that could not be generated by either firm in isolation and can only be created through the specialized inputs of both alliance partners – is a function of investment and learning. These complementary resource investments are fully combined, are not available outside of the partnership and, most important, are extremely difficult for competitors to imitate. The benefits derived from these unique partnerships provide both strategic and organizational returns and a powerful source of competitive advantage. Yet, despite these significant potential gains, partnerships frequently fail to live up to their initial promise.

The missing element is perhaps the most critical and the most difficult to pin down. The very act of partnering leads to an increase in complexity and a lack of autonomy that are fundamental aspects of working with other firms. These fundamentals, which are at odds with the experience of most managers ('command and control'), can be obstacles to the achievement of the gains that a partnership represents. This is exacerbated by increased misunderstandings, poor communication and limited information-sharing, which can 'eat' into the very heart of the relationship.

This is the partnering conundrum. Partnerships offer major benefits but at a cost: a firm loses some control, it gains another management challenge, and it will know even less about its partner's operations than it does about its own business. This is compounded by the lack of general managerial experience in partnering and an absence of diagnostic tools and metrics to manage the relationship on anything other than raw outputs.

These difficulties can be mitigated by a firm's ability to seek out and nurture suitable potential partners in the first place and to create and operate within an environment of complementary organizational systems, processes and cultures. This leads to a situation where assets can be leveraged and learning can be captured. Subsequently, and if appropriate, the partnership can be terminated efficiently and effectively once the objectives have been captured and realized. This is the management task and as such these activities are considered to be part of good governance because they impact both transaction costs and value creation. Thus governance is a multidimensional phenomenon that encompasses the beginning, ending and ongoing relationship management between a set of parties. The governance or management of the partnership or alliance therefore:

- influences a firm's willingness and ability to cooperate and therefore to leverage its investments;

- provides a foundation stone for establishing a learning environment;

- offers the vehicle for a reduction of information asymmetry;
- explicitly confronts and addresses the issues of complexity and lack of autonomy.

Dell's partnering policy

Underpinning the success that Dell enjoys is the closeness of the relationships with its suppliers and the approach taken in their management. A fundamental plank of Michael Dell's original strategy is the belief that it was better to partner with suppliers of PC parts and components rather than to integrate backward and get into parts and components manufacturing in its own right.

Dell can identify several benefits it gained through its approach:

- It adopted a limited supplier strategy and worked only with those firms that could demonstrate leadership in technology, which led to enhanced quality and performance of Dell's PCs.
- Dell made a commitment to each supplier that it would purchase a specified percentage of its requirements from each. This meant that in an often turbulent marketplace, Dell was practically guaranteed to get the components it needed, when and where it needed them.
- Dell invited its suppliers into its product development process, which meant that they were on hand during critical launch periods to resolve any technical or quality issues.
- Dell provided its suppliers with a 'window' into the manufacturing or assembly process so that they could better plan their own production.
- Dell shared critical information with its suppliers on a real-time basis. A monthly forecast was complemented by a closed information loop that provided both Dell's manufacturing with product availability details, and suppliers with the 'pull' or demand on parts.

This was not an arm's length relationship, and although suppliers might not appreciate the high levels of service levels that Dell expected, they could not argue that they didn't know what was required of them.

The influence of leadership and control mechanisms

Overlapping this discussion on governance is the consideration of control methods. There are two basic approaches to controlling partnerships. The first is external and emphasizes the use of formal rules, procedures and policies to monitor and reward desirable performance. The second is internal and relies on establishing social norms of behaviour. By accommodating the different values and cultures of the parties it is possible for people to identify with the common goals of the alliance, to build personal ties and overcome opportunistic temptations. This has often been called 'clan control' and is commonly associated with collaborative relationships. Formal and social/informal control systems are not mutually exclusive and much has been written on the effects of culture and social mechanisms within organizations. These typically use rewards and formal control mechanisms such as performance-related pay. For instance, manufacturing firms will provide intermediaries with performance-based rewards and accreditation programmes in order to incentivize appropriate behaviours. Formal or informal controls should not be associated with any particular type of operational structure, eg from discrete to highly integrated, and variations and combinations will be found depending on the specific situation within most organizations.

Both types of control have arguments for and against their use. It has been suggested that appropriate formal controls may support the development of reliable relationships that are not emotive, have objective performance measures and rules, and are both open and honest. In contrast, the presence of rules and regulations may imply mistrust or the limitation of flexibility. In consequence, personal innovation may be diminished as may the credibility of either per-formance- or behaviour-based reward systems.

Irrespective of the governance form that is adopted, or the manage-ment systems that are put in place to direct the processes, firms can also be differentiated in terms of the leadership style they adopt. Leadership methods focus on ways in which a leader can effectively bring about collaboration as well as compliance from subordinates. In the context of partnering and in particular in networks, consortia and marketing channels, one firm will emerge that will attempt to act as the leader or 'channel captain'. For many years researchers into marketing channels were preoccupied with the issues of control and power, ie the ability to dominate and exert influence. However, these ideas ignored the benefits that could be achieved through non-coercive leadership styles. Three particular leadership styles can be considered:

1. *Participative* – participative leaders share a significant degree of decision-making power with their subordinates. In the marketing channels setting, a participative leader would consult with channel participants and actively solicit their suggestions for use in making decisions on the design and introduction of channel-wide policies and procedures.

2. *Supportive* – a supportive channel leader would consider other channel participants' needs, take note of their accomplishments, look out for their welfare, attempt to establish mutual interest and build a 'team climate'.

3. *Directive* – the directive channel leader assigns the necessary distri-bution tasks to be performed, specifies the rules, regulations and procedures to be followed, clarifies expectations, schedules work to be done, establishes communication networks and evaluates channel member performance.

As with modes of governance, there is 'no right way' for particular channel or partnership configuration. Perhaps the directive mode is seen as the most common leadership type in use. However, given that the objectives of alliance or channel leadership are to influence the policies and strategies of other members, it is more likely that leaders will exhibit varying degrees of participative, directional or supportive leadership styles simultaneously.

Understanding partnership performance

If you can't measure it you can't manage it and, what doesn't get measured doesn't get done.

(Attributed to Andrew Grove, Chairman and co-founder of Intel Corp)

Collaborative relationships start out as clear structures but rapidly become more complex. A number of factors can drive this complexity as, for example, their physical features develop and adapt, as processes change, as people modify and add their own individuality to working practices, and as commercial frameworks and IT systems attempt to keep pace. Knowledge gaps may open up between the various management levels, between functions, and between the interfacing elements of the partnering companies. Traditional management techniques that focus on 'supplier management' (a one-way view) are likely to find themselves blinkered and prevented from understanding the key aspects of joint, complex relationship management, which demands a reciprocal perspective.

Firms in this position usually concentrate on managing their relationships by high-level time, cost and quality objectives – basic operational metrics focusing on the inputs and outputs. In doing so they forget that a more hands-on, joint approach is needed to get the best out of a necessarily close and mutually confined situation. In consequence the minor issues that result from inter-organizational frictions do not become apparent until they have become serious enough to penetrate the traditional management information systems (such as balanced scorecard, six sigma and project management) at which time reactive fire-fighting has begun and the contract is being examined for penalty clauses. For many firms, managing the relationship only becomes an agenda item when the partnership is already in disarray. Even more worrying, this approach often fails to see the joint opportunities that emerge to make processes more efficient, to improve products and services and to seize new market openings. This aspect of partnering management is insidious as firms rarely recognize the opportunities they have missed until it is too late

Table 3.1 Partnership governance

Poor Relationship Performance	High Relationship Performance
Poor relationship management	Proactive relationship
Lack of commitment	management
Adversarial practices	Joint objectives
Inadequate joint performance	High-level commitment
measurement	No-blame culture
Fear of dependency	Visibility of performance
	measurements
	Joint planning
	Open communication

to capture them – or not at all. The issues are summarized in Table 3.1. A number of negative practices and illustrative quotations from managers drawn from research follow.

Poor management of the relationship

The prime cause of poor performance in collaborative business relationships is the underestimation of the management task. Companies often do what they know best, run operations, but are usually either ignorant of or under-resource the 'choreography' of complex, inter-organizational dealings:

'We often have great problems contacting the customer's project managers.'
'At the middle-management level of the supplier the message has not hit home and the same old culture and practices prevail.'
'They seem unable to understand that one point of contact is inadequate to deal with the multi-level issues that occur.'
'We just don't have time to take a strategic view; we are too busy looking after 30 other contracts.'

Lack of commitment

Lack of commitment is often manifested in inadequate joint planning, investment, staffing and management structures:

'We get more information about their future policy and plans from their website than from them face-to-face.'
'They show no sign of wanting to do better; their management is so self-satisfied.'
'We have tried hard to improve the relationship using in-house resources but now that we have run out we are getting no support from the corporate HQ.'

Adversarial practices

Adversarial and bureaucratic commercial practices that result in 'them and us' attitudes, poor quality communications and selfish behaviours cause increased costs and delays and reduce trust:

'They have no "faces". They are known as "they". We have no shared view of what we are delivering. Even an annual review would be welcome.'
'Their view of sharing is they have the lion's share and we get what's left over.'
'In one instance they billed us for defective packaging and then refused to help resolve the problem with the supplier.'
'We fear and mistrust a shared data environment because it gives our customer the opportunity to "hit us over the head".'
'They have done this often in the past.'

Inadequate joint performance measurement

Poor joint performance measures and systems result in incompatible objectives, disjointed processes, poor quality, higher costs and low customer service:

'I am concerned at our lack of touch with the end-customers. We need seamless performance measurement throughout the logistics chain.'

'We know our own targets and objectives well but those of our supply chain partners are a mystery. We certainly don't have any common targets.'

'We don't have joint performance measures as such. We send them a monthly return of test yields but they give no feedback.'

'Although we have notional joint performance objectives, getting service out of our partner is like getting "poop" from a rocking-horse.'

Fear of dependency

In a collaborative business relationship each party's freedom of action is necessarily reduced, and they may have feelings of uncertainty and risk because they are dependent on each other. There is a very real danger of small issues becoming bigger ones, and the onset of an adversarial mindset can start a downward spiral:

'Over the last five years we have "ticked" along with one product. We are working jointly to release a new product next year. This will really put the relationship to the test because we are totally dependent on them for its success.'

'Unfortunately the coherence of the programme lost its way over time. It lost touch with reality and became a monthly shouting match.'

'They want us to bend the rules all the time and our failure to do so is seen as inflexible and unfriendly.'

'Their attitude is, "We'll share whatever you have got".'

A majority of the obstacles that hinder good partnership working are thus caused by poor understanding of the important performance drivers within a specific relationship situation. This is often due to the inability of senior managers to have a current, objective view of the joint enterprise that is unclouded by the usual complexity and time delays.

It is possible to identify best practices that drive successful relationships. Our research has shown that effective relationships are often characterized by a number of positive practices. These can be illustrated by the following quotations from managers drawn from our research.

Joint objectives

The commercial framework for the collaboration must provide tough but achievable joint objectives and clear incentives for value creation:

'The key is to harmonize the main objectives. Others that are not important and act as obstructions must be identified and suppressed.'
'The new partnering arrangement will run over 10 years and includes gain-share arrangements.'
'We can now leave the contract behind us and concentrate together on the output to the customer.'
'This constant development creates value; we don't chase each other but we do challenge each other.'
'We like to see each company grow. That's special. You don't see that in many relationships.'

Visibility of performance measures

The parties to the relationship must have clear sight of the end-to-end performance requirements of all supply chain players including the end-customers, so that overall efficiency is pursued:

'Everybody has a good understanding of the performance measures. We all participated in setting them up.'
'We jointly work to a clear programme plan where we regularly review our achievements and plan ahead.'
'Information flows are very well established and regimented. This ensures there are no ambiguities over performance expectations.'

Open communication

Frequent, interactive, open communication across all levels of the customer/supplier interface, especially on performance reviews and continuous improvement of products/services and business processes, is essential, especially when dealing with unexpected problems:

'Every month a project meeting is held where red flag issues on health and safety, costs and quality are raised. These are minuted and dates for remedial action are specified.'

'We have simple, obvious, open performance measures. Every week the supplier sends us a statement of work achieved, problems and forecasts, and we pass them consumption data. The achievements are open for all to see.'

'We are very innovative and have lots of ideas about how we can do things better. For example, we built tests into the product and achieved a 98 per cent pass rate compared to 30 per cent previously. As a team we worked really well.'

'There were good joint discussions on successes and failures to learn from, and then come up with solutions to fix problems.'

No-blame culture and trust

An open, no-blame culture aimed at customer and relationship satisfaction, which depends on personal, trusting relationships, will ensure that the parties focus on the main joint objectives and do not get bogged down in trivial, but often emotive, self-interested issues:

'The trust that has built up over the years is a result of working together to achieve the desired end.'

'If our partners fall down I want to know why; however, if it's a genuine problem we will make every effort to help them resolve it, including asking the client for extra money.'

'Our relationship is very open, frank and understanding with lots of mutual respect. We learn from each other.'

'Time and time again they have "pulled out the stops" to help us solve unexpected snags. We will certainly "go the extra mile" for them.'

Joint planning

Joint planning and business systems supported by free-flowing information will provide a flexible, efficient, collaborative operation to meet market demands:

'Quarterly review meetings where outstanding orders are discussed have led to improved availability.'

'By having a member of staff in their team we are able to communicate much better, reduce misunderstandings, and gain a much clearer idea of the plans for the business.'

'All support chain parties, including the end-customer, attend planning meetings to discuss requirements, pool knowledge and resolve problems.'

'I tell the supplier honestly my budget for the coming year so he can plan ahead.'

'We get as much forward planning information as they can give us. There is a lot of "out of the blue" work and we must be flexible.'

High-level commitment

A constant focus on high-level objectives will result in success that reinforces success; in effect countering any negative behavioural tendencies and generating an upward success spiral:

'Now that we have a partnering arrangement around a good framework contract we just concentrate on the customer – we no longer refer to the small print.'

'The partnership has gone from strength to strength as we have overcome problems, met our milestones and achieved success.'

'With some trepidation we asked our parts supplier to help us design the new product. We have been amazed. The product is now cheaper, more reliable and contains more features and is loved by our customers. Our relationship has blossomed as a result.'

Proactive relationship management

It has already been noted that traditional management practices inherently become more reactive in the face of increasing complexity. The pattern in Figure 3.1 is very common.

Periodically management decide that the problems have accumulated to such a point that the only option is to 'blitz' the situation. This usually involves bringing in consultants at considerable expense and disruption. The work will focus on the 'issues' and the

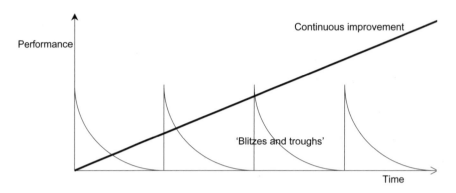

Figure 3.1 The 'blitz' approach to change

implementation plan will take considerable time to institutionalize. Almost immediately performance will begin to drop off until the 'blitz' has to be repeated. The solution is to adopt a more proactive, joint approach to relationship management that focuses on addressing both strengths and weaknesses and achieves continuous improvement. This requires a consistent focus on change management: change management in the context of building relationship management into partnering is a critical element for success. Figure 3.2 shows a relationship management cycle that not only increases control but also ensures that improvement is continuous.

Adapt

Change may be required for either internal or external reasons, but in any organization it is usually difficult to achieve, even if it is urgently required. Not only are people and systems resistant but also the business disruption, cost and management effort are daunting. In a partnering situation the challenge is more than doubled. Only by building consensus around the joint benefits that can be achieved will effective headway be made. This requires joint ownership at both senior and local levels of the projects that must be defined and put into practice if headway is to be made.

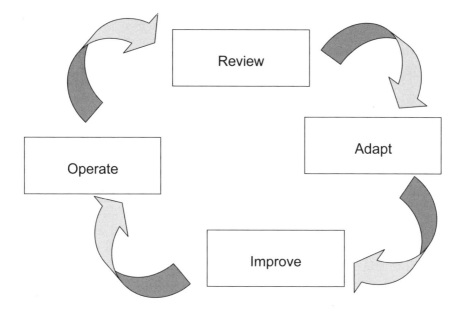

Figure 3.2 The relationship management cycle

Improve

Traditionally firms focused on seeking out problems and solving them, and used management information systems that were designed to highlight inefficiencies. More modern, quality system approaches contain a new emphasis on seeking out processes that can be further improved. Many organizations form partnering arrangements without considering how these important functions will be handled. It is essential that shared views of the relationship's performance are created and joint mechanisms are put in place that will manage problem solving and relationship improvement.

Operate

Many organizations fail to meet frequently to review performance and plan ahead. Every important relationship should invest in a regular (probably monthly) operational review meeting, attended by the 'movers and shakers' on each side, which as a minimum does the following:

- review performance targets in the last period and issue statistics;
- review work/orders in progress;
- review forecasted sales and orders in the next period;
- consider and solve problems;
- review future plans (including new products) and initiate preparation;
- review industry and technology updates;
- identify policy.

At its heart this operational process should actively seek out and initiate process improvements. It should be the forum where issues are jointly raised with senior management and where recommended corrective actions are developed. This group should 'nip problems in the bud', adapt the relationship to change in a timely way, and be the first to highlight new relationship opportunities.

Review

Most organizations and relationships will have a plethora of detailed performance measures that will need to be tuned to encompass the end-to-end aspects of the supply chain relationships. However, this is not enough to ensure success. More comprehensive measures of 'relationship' performance, which combine contract fulfilment with the achievement of wider joint values, need to be embraced. Many partners feel insecure because of their lack of overview of relationship performance, which causes them to maintain an unhealthy preoccupation with the contract 'small print'. In contrast, relationship performance measurement shifts the focus firmly onto customer satisfaction by creating, maintaining and building joint understanding that places quality, innovation, communication, cost reductions, on-time delivery, commitment, the future and trust at the centre of the partners' attention. Finally, just as with conventional performance measurement, relationship performance measurement must include objective metrics that allow joint progress to be measured and targets to be set. More will be said on this subject in later chapters.

Summary

This chapter has reviewed the main factors that affect the performance of inter-organizational relationships. It has described how investments by partnership members create the unique combination that generates competitive advantage and, importantly, cement the relationship by building trust and commitment. Underpinning this is the importance of learning from alliance partners and being able to use this as a benefits multiplier to the advantage of the firm and of the partnership. The ability to manage relationships and deal with appropriate governance structures, control mechanisms and leadership styles has also been considered because this is a critical factor in reducing confrontation, building trust and collaboration and ensuring the ongoing maintenance of the partnership. The chapter has also reviewed the practical management challenges represented by understanding actual performance and being able to act on this information proactively. It concluded that effective relationship performance measurement was key to realizing relationship success; however, the detail of how this can be put into practice will be covered in later chapters.

Table 3.2 Assessing your partnership behaviours

Poor Behaviours	−3	−2	−1	0	+1	+2	+3	Good Behaviours
Poor management of the relationship								No-blame culture and trust
Lack of commitment								High-level commitment
Adversarial practices								Joint objectives/open communication
Inadequate joint performance measurement								Visibility of performance measures
Fear of interdependency								Joint planning

Key action points

1. Taking all things into consideration, how would you rate your performance in managing partnerships?

2. How would your current and most recent partners describe your partnering maturity?

3. List five investments that your firm has made in your partnerships that have/have not yielded the desired outcomes.

4. What factors have determined whether these investments were 'successful' or not?

5. List five things that your partnerships have taught you in the last five years.

6. What changes to your processes, etc have come about as a consequence of learning from your partnerships?

7. What 'in-process' metrics do you apply to your partnering management?

8. How would you describe your typical partner management style: participative, supportive or directive?

9. Considering your partnership(s), how would you assess your firm along the scales shown in Table 3.2?

10. To what extent do you follow adapt, improve, operate and review steps in your partner management?

4 Relationship marketing: a 'new-old' theory of business relationships

Marketing is too important to be left to the marketing department.

(David Packard, co-founder of Hewlett-Packard)

Marketing foundations

One of the earlier forms of marketing was 'managerial marketing'. This emphasized discrete transactions, planning, control and profit maximization and its primary focus was the 'exchange relationship' with the aim of allowing anything except 'killing and stealing'. This approach thrived in large organizations in the 1970s and 1980s and complemented the then prevalent assertive sales management style and reinforced the standard adversarial mode of doing business. The European Industrial Marketing Group (IMP) led by Hakan Hakansson in the mid 1980s, saw things differently. It took the 'no man is an island' view that firms no longer stood alone against the 'opposition' and that adversarial sales management might not be the only or even the best option. Instead a firm could form value-added partnerships within networks of industrial relationships with the intention of managing the flows of goods and services around specific market opportunities. These relationships were complex and often very close. Furthermore, they were recognized as valuable resources and investments in their own right that had the potential to increase returns, improve efficiency, provide an important source of learning and reduce risk.

At the same time as the increased attention on and growth in strategic alliances and partnering during the 1990s, a major new change in direction was taking place in both marketing theory and practice. This was the rediscovery of 'relationship marketing'. This chapter looks at how this apparently 'new' marketing concept shifted management's view from the short-term, arm's length way of doing business to one that realized the importance of partnerships and actively explored this new, collaborative way of working. Whilst spurring relationship managers to win out against the traditionalists, there was also considerable interest in understanding and modelling partnerships in order to give managers the information with which to improve their performance. This soon led to the notion that above average management of a 'partnership' could produce above average returns. This chapter concludes by considering three 'generations' of partnering excellence.

Relationship marketing rediscovered

Marketing guru Philip Kotler described relationship marketing (RM) as a 'new-old concept' because it was not so much a discovery but a rediscovery of an approach that had long been the cornerstone of many successful businesses. Nevertheless, RM remains a difficult concept to pin down and has been said to cover as diverse a set of ideas as relational contracting, relational marketing, buyer/seller relationships, working partnerships, collaborative relationships and strategic alliances. According to other commentators it focuses on integrating quality management, services marketing and customer relationship economics in one 'all-pervasive paradigm'. Central to RM is an orientation towards longer-term customer retention through continuous and frequent customer contact (both pre- and post-sale), with an accompanying increase in the importance attached to service and quality.

The underlying logic of customer retention is unassailable and the real benefits of retained customers over new customers are as follows:

- The costs of acquiring new customers can be substantial. A higher retention rate implies that fewer customers need to be acquired.

- Established customers tend to buy more.

- Regular customers place frequent, consistent orders and therefore usually cost less to serve.

- Satisfied customers often refer new customers to the supplier at virtually no cost.

- Satisfied customers are often willing to pay premium prices for a supplier they know and trust.

- Retaining customers makes market entry or share gain difficult for competitors.

With marketing's focus shifting away from merely attracting customers to those activities that concern having customers and taking care of them – the 'customer franchise' – a new set of challenges arose. The customer franchise was broader, it was more sophisticated and demanding and it couldn't be satisfied with a narrow offering. RM needed to reconnect all a firm's functions with the single aim of meeting customers' expectations. After all, the brand image isn't just the name of a product or company: it represents the carefully conceived array of all activities both pre- and post-sale that make the buyer recognize its unique added value compared with the competing products and services. The objective of the customer franchise and cumulative image is to get and significantly to maintain a loyal customer base. Moreover, it is essential to do this in the most cost-effective manner to achieve the highest possible return on investment.

It was soon recognized that firms needed not only to align their own resources, but to fully succeed they needed to enhance the total offering. It was also recognized that this could not be done without the full cooperation and support of all the essential suppliers, the intermediaries and the partners whose roles were now seen as contributory and adding value. As a result RM not only generated a critical focus on the customers' satisfaction but also drove firms to expand the RM concept to fully embrace the establishment, development and maintenance of the long-term relationships with these key enabling partners – see Figure 4.1. This was a very broad remit that extended well beyond the usual responsibilities of the marketing department and, in fact, extended right across the whole organization and a range of stakeholders such as suppliers, marketing intermediaries, the public and, of course, to the customers who were the most important link in the chain.

Out of this 'revolutionary' approach has emerged a new vocabulary that includes long-term customer orientation, mutual dependence, trust, cooperation, social relationships, social responsibility and customer value creation. These have transformed strategic advantage discussions away from the original confines of transactional costs, product advantages or benchmark operation to see competitive advantage as spanning the processes and routines between the firm and its partners. Thus, while 'keeping your customer satisfied' is an old adage, the new RM paradigm forced firms to extend its scope to all participants in the supply chain.

Collaborate or fail

The relatively recent re-recognition of the importance of RM by firms brought with it a realization of the implications of pursuing such a customer value creation strategy. It was clear that the creation and delivery of customer value was too great a burden for one firm acting independently and that it needed to collaborate with others

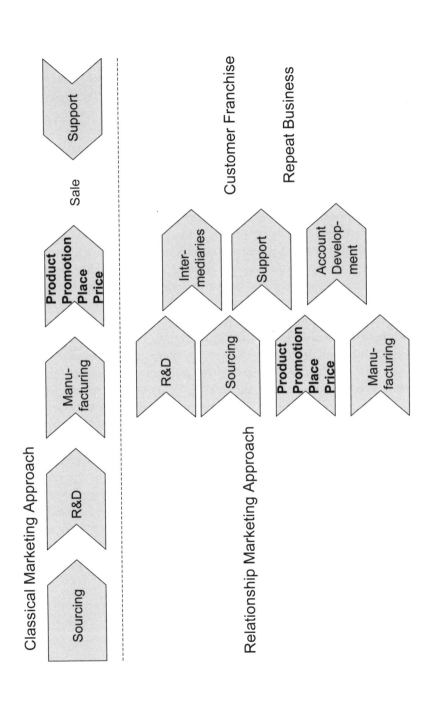

Figure 4.1 The relationship marketing paradigm shift

to deliver and fulfil these exacting requirements. Furthermore, this idea of value creation through collaboration rather than simple transactions depended on serious cooperation using a web of operational and interpersonal connections and structures. RM therefore forced many firms to recognize that to be an effective 'competitor' (in the global economy) requires one to be a trusted 'cooperator' (in some network).

In the past, collaboration has not been a typical element of the commercial psyche within Fortune 500 organizations. It has been likened to 'working with the enemy' (the alternative definition of collaboration) and this mindset, together with the lack of suitable skills, has compounded partnership underperformance. As an alternative to the Anglo/US competitive and often adversarial style of business relationships, the Japanese *keiretsu* model proposes avoiding confrontation as the main way of solving disputes. This requires closer long-term relationships between buyers and sellers but the result is an ability to create greater value than either of the parties could achieve individually.

As such, firms wishing to fully capitalize on the benefits of partnerships to address the needs of their customers need to adopt the RM way of doing business towards the partners themselves, otherwise they are unlikely to be successful. At the same time, where firms are able to collaborate with their partners they will be in a position to start to earn extraordinary profits, so called 'relational rents'. These 'rents' are the benefits that accrue over and above the expected performance as a direct consequence of the efficiency and effectiveness with which firms work together. At this point the critical importance to firms of collaborating successfully becomes crystal clear. If you don't collaborate, a firm won't be able to address the needs of its customers. If you don't collaborate well, a firm won't reap the relationship benefits that can form the basis of competitive advantage.

From power management to relationship management

Relational marketing strategies have gradually supplanted more dictatorial, aggressive modes of dealing with partners. However, there continues to be a debate using the economic arguments on the need to take more positive, authoritarian approaches to control within relationships. This is, it is proposed, because ultimately it is necessary, given the considerations of stewardships and accountability to shareholders, to use contracts to enforce obligations and because it is logical and prudent to be distrustful (male-dominated environment and norms). Thus if a firm has earned the upper hand, the argument goes, power must be exerted to ensure that it gets the returns it deserves regardless of its impact on its partners: 'They, after all, should look after themselves; it's a tough world out there.' Within the supply chain partnership theories of the 1980s, this was known as 'gaining the high ground', but it tended to cause a destructive pursuit of lowest cost, which led to low quality and value that eventually had a destructive impact on the firm and the industry. These impacts were reflected in other partnerships, such as strategic alliances which were conditioned and managed through extensive legal contracts, and marketing channels that were driven ('carrot and stick') by overly aggressive manufacturers.

However, the shift to RM has been further accelerated as a consequence of mounting concerns over these potential negative outcomes of managing partnerships through the use of force or penalizing contracts. Simultaneously, changes in industry structures, patterns of dependency and sources of power have made it more difficult for the established 'robber barons' to hold court and demand acquiescence. In this respect RM promoted the establishment of agreed standards of behaviour where firms consider the intrinsic importance of the relationship and thus look to avoid taking actions that jeopardize its continuity. In contrast to market forces, 'command and control' or hierarchical structures of governance, this fresh approach is akin to the 'clan mechanism' where the partners adopt the expected social behavioural norms of the alliance and deal with problems in a self-controlled fashion.

Two important drivers reinforced the importance of this approach. On the one hand there is the need for firms to work together to improve efficiency in increasingly complex supply chains involving numerous intermediaries. On the other, alliances can confront global competition, product and operational parity, and address shifting and more complex customer needs.

Set in the above context it is apparent that cooperation is more likely to achieve these aims because it is inherently more flexible and creative than the traditional adversarial methods. RM has thus now become a prime reason for firms to build a long-term association, characterized by resolute cooperation, mutual reliance and both social and structural linkages.

The relationship business

Doing business from a relationship perspective thus seems to represent the best strategy to follow in today's business climate; however, it is important that this paradigm shift is put into practice and is not simply a case of lip-service being paid to a new trend. To illustrate the components and potential transitions, marketing relationships can be described as a set of stages that progress from open market purchases with no relational content to the other extreme of vertical integration where all is controlled under one firm's 'roof'. This is shown in Figure 4.2.

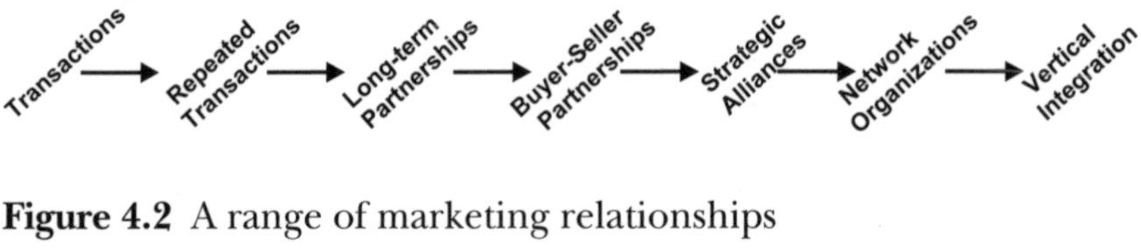

Transactions → Repeated Transactions → Long-term Partnerships → Buyer-Seller Partnerships → Strategic Alliances → Network Organizations → Vertical Integration

Figure 4.2 A range of marketing relationships

Each step is linked to the next by building the appropriate conditions for the transition. As firms (and their corresponding relationships) move along the scale there is a need for greater bureaucratic and administrative control because of the increasing complexity and lower influence of price. Pure market transactions are generally driven by price and availability, but when they are repeated the subsequent engagement is conditioned by the previous experience and 'consciously' sets the foundation for the next episode. In a buyer-seller relationship it is likely that the seller will acknowledge this repetitive activity by offering price-breaks and other incentives, but the firm may not always know its repeat customers by name unless, for instance, something significant like volume comes into play. Suppliers will usually analyse their sales statistics and identify their key customers and make special efforts to tailor incentives or initiatives using key account management techniques. They hope that they will turn these relationships into long-term ones and the idea of mutually beneficial enterprise begins to arise.

Partnerships therefore occur when either the customer or supplier develops a concept that requires some form of customization in form or delivery. They will both contribute some type of investment such as finance and know-how to produce and sell a unique product or service. In doing so they will become dependent on each other for their contribution and as a result will build up trust in each other. At this point, the ability of a contract to adequately cover the complexities of the arrangement becomes questionable and the partners will realize that penalty clauses and litigation would do more harm than good.

This initial period of exploration and forming is followed by the management of the relationship being seen as an activity in itself and a partnership is born. The difference between this type of partnership and a strategic alliance is difficult to see, particularly in smaller firms where a close partnership can take on a strategic significance. When firms form a strategic alliance, each commits major (relative) resources toward a strategic or otherwise vital objective. In the case of construction firm AMEC and civil engineering designer Halcrow, their collaboration included some major projects such as the M62 motorway and the London Docklands Light Railway, which spanned seven years.

When firms come together in multiple relationships, partnerships, or strategic alliances, the resultant structure is a network organization. Given the global nature of modern products, their development, distribution and sales, network organizations are much more prevalent than even five years ago. Many electronics products such as the games consoles of Sony and Microsoft are designed in the US, manufactured in the Far East (with components sourced widely) and distributed through an extensive range of intermediary chains to sales outlets in virtually every country in the world.

The ultimate marketing relationship is vertical integration where all relationships are controlled within a single, conglomerate organization. However, this type of business – like the Ford Motor Company of the early 20th century described in Chapter 1 – is no longer either fashionable or practical because it is insufficiently flexible, excessively massive and unable to develop or manage the sort of innovation needed in today's business world.

Traditionally businesses saw their power as the key to maintaining order and control in alliances. Instead, and bearing in mind that roughly one-third of ventures such as strategic alliances are outright failures, our research has shown that placing a central focus on RM has a significant positive impact on the partnership. In this way it is possible to understand and determine what distinguishes productive, effective, relational exchanges from those that are unproductive and ineffective. The relationship business therefore contains both social and historical aspects because it expects its members to live up to their side of the bargain, to understand that memories are long, especially in cases of bad behaviour and, as a member of the clan or partnership, to share common goals and objectives.

Modelling the marketing relationship

The marketing relationship can be better understood and measured by exploring three key components of partnership business:

1. Trust and commitment.

2. Conflict management.

3. Collaboration.

Each of these plays a significant role in determining the quality of the relationship as well as influencing the tangible and critical outcomes of the partnership in terms of partner satisfaction and performance.

1. Trust and commitment

Both trust and commitment are generally accepted as essential requirements for successful partnerships; they remain important throughout the entire partner lifecycle from start to finish. The overall level of trust is represented by the extent to which a partner believes that a firm will consider its needs and requirements when setting and deploying its strategies and policies. For instance, the establishment of a new pricing policy that raises volume thresholds beyond that achievable by many channel partners will reduce the level of trust in a relationship. Reliability is an important factor and is one part of the 'walking the talk', ie whether the firm will actually do what it says it will do and deliver on its stated commitments and promises. Another is the reputation and credibility of the firm to deliver on its promises, ie can the firm actually do what it says it will? Does the partner have the confidence that a firm has the skills and competences necessary for the partnership to be successful?

Sometimes it takes a bit of a 'leap in faith' to trust a business partner, especially when the relationship is new and there is little experience of working together. This risk needs to be evaluated carefully, but really strong team-working is likely to develop from a cycle of small, confidence-building projects that establish trust as a virtuous cycle. In essence, when a party has the belief and confidence that the other will act reliably, with integrity, in the best interests of the partnership, then trust is present. There is little doubt that the demonstration of the various forms of trust, risk-taking and successful fulfilment of expectations will strengthen the willingness of the parties to rely on each other and, as a result, expand the partnership.

Trust often goes hand-in-hand with commitment, which can be thought of as following on from the perceived importance of the partnership. Typically commitment can be viewed as the motivation and willingness of a firm to see a long-term relationship with its partner(s) as something that is worthwhile and important. The partners may have common goals that they could not achieve separately. One firm may lack a key ingredient, a skill, resource or capability, and need the help of the other. A powerful source of commitment is the significant revenue, profit or other value that a partner can capture from the alliance that spurs it to want the relationship to continue.

Trust and commitment are thus key indicators of whether an alliance will be sustained and developed over time and are directly linked to the level of satisfaction measured in traditional customer satisfaction (CSAT) surveys. Without trust and commitment, firms will find it difficult to create the conditions that enable knowledge to be shared and transferred between them. Trust and commitment are also important in terms of the ability of a partnership to realize or capture the value that is created through the partnership. The trustworthiness of the partner and the relative importance of the partnership are enhanced by the investment in key resources that both the partner and the firm make. These investments have been thought of as pledges or signals that the relationship has a substantive raison d'etre which strengthens commitment. Organizations that enjoy high levels of trust and commitment will see channel partners making full use of the programmes and initiatives that the host firm makes available. Conversely, where trust and commitment are low then the likelihood is that the recipient firm will treat the relationship as a short-lived opportunity and as a consequence either 'cherry pick' opportunities for collaboration or even enter into direct competition with alternative brands in target accounts.

2. Conflict management

The management of conflict is a very important factor in building an effective working partnership. It is thus useful to understand the potential sources of conflict that could undermine performance.

Conflict arises when the aims of partners are not compatible and when the rationale for the relationship in terms of the partners agreeing the common purpose and objectives of working together is misaligned. To avoid this fundamental source of friction there is a need to develop synergy and common interests between the firms to set the direction of the relationship from the start and provide the forward momentum as the common objectives are translated into mutually agreed targets. Allied to the need to establish the clear joint objectives of the alliance is the need to maintain them as conditions change. For instance, the overall go-to-market design (channels and alliances), policies and strategies that the firm operates will need to be continually renegotiated and adapted. If this does not happen then destructive disagreements arise that are frequent, intense and often provide the grounds to terminate the partnership.

Operational problems are bound to occur; this is in the nature of any complex, collaborative enterprise. However, given that trust and commitment are essential drivers to success, the accumulation of 'rankles' and 'frictions' must not be allowed to subvert the alliance. It is thus crucial to have in place procedures to deal with them quickly, openly and fairly.

Not all conflict, however, is bad. 'Good conflict' can be thought of as when partners feel able to challenge one another. This can lead to heated and sometimes uncomfortable meetings, but this type of conflict can be the source of innovation and creativity as an agreed position emerges. In benchmark partnerships, the common purpose and goals that avoid destructive conflict and enable constructive conflict are complemented and supported by the firms' broader strategies and polices. These ensure that return on investment is optimized and the disruption caused by conflict is turned into opportunities to increase partnership performance. Thus, conflict management is the key driver to relationship performance in terms of the tangible process outcomes of revenue, market share, customer retention and capture.

3. Collaboration

Collaboration is both critical to the efficient management of the partnership and in determining the level of performance within a relationship. Collaborative activity is dependent upon efficient coordination and planning, which requires effective communication and efficient cooperative activities. A common failing of many partnerships is the overt focus on establishing a list of cooperative actions such as joint sales engagements with prospects without the essential prior discussion and planning.

In RM, collaboration is a key driver to the scale of joint business achievable and is associated with improved ROI as well as reducing conflict and building trust and commitment. Collaboration results from a shift away from the 'account management' mindset to one of 'business management'. This must include suppliers and inter-mediaries as well as customers. As a consequence of this shift it is important to recognize that alliance and partner managers require

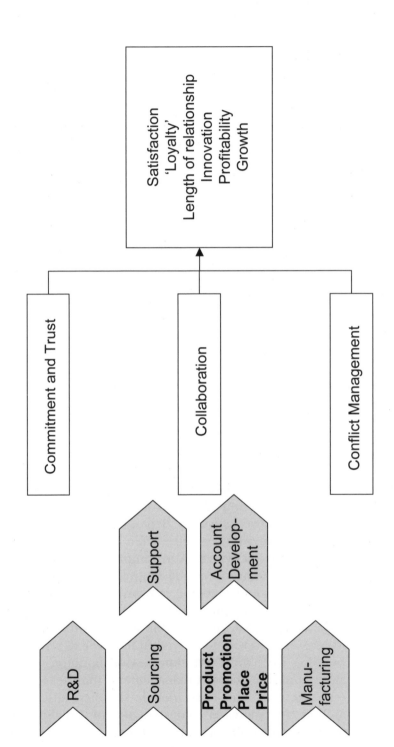

Figure 4.3 Components of relationship management

different skills from sales managers. These business management skills are essential to effective collaboration. Within successful collaborative organizations there are practiced processes and procedures and an established structure that allows knowledge and expertise to be collected and transferred through syndicates, workshops and networks on best practices for partner communication, coordination and cooperation. The breakdown of the essential behaviour components of a partnership using RM ideas is shown in Figure 4.3.

All the practical aspects of managing joint operations depend for their performance on the pivotal relationship factors and these – commitment and trust, collaboration and conflict management – enable the objectives of the alliance to be met. It thus now becomes possible to start to develop metrics to evaluate each, to weigh and measure the considered views of partnership people, to understand their interactions, and to start to determine which 'levers' change what in the managers' 'control panel' to achieve success.

Leveraging the relationship to re-energize a new channel

The last decade has seen a clear trend of firms expanding their routes to market in order to increase their coverage of end-customer segments. For the firm in this case study, this strategic decision was taken in Europe in 2000 and over the next 18 months partners were recruited through a series of successful marketing programmes. The firm is a large multinational organization within the Forbes Top 500 corporations, whose European sales channels traditionally included direct sales and franchises, and as such the decision to increase its routes to market was bold and strategic.

The IT Reseller Channel was a success in 2000 and 2001. The opening up of the firm's products to the independent channel was proving a winner with little actual conflict towards the established channels and no proven cannibalization of the businesses. The results for 2001 were good: 750 IT partners produced substantial growth for the new channel, sales targets were over-achieved and satisfaction ratings were high. Over 1,000 IT resellers traded in 2002, but the value of their business was decreasing year-on-year. Initially this was put down to a consequence of falling price points and the launch of an entry-level product, but this trend continued in 2003 despite various programmes to raise the average purchase value. Revenue stabilized slightly but little growth was apparent. The firm responded with a series of reseller recruitment campaigns in the belief that the initial selection process had been flawed. These proved partially successful. New partners were trading but this was counter-balanced by existing resellers reducing or ceasing selling the firm's products. Repeat purchases from new resellers failed to materialize over subsequent months after the initial recruitment.

Early in 2003 operational quality research was conducted that revealed that IT resellers were satisfied with the core offering of the vendor. In fact satisfaction with the product, brand strength and profitability was increasing. Purchase experience was also good. Research also indicated that resellers were satisfied to the extent that they wanted to resell the firm's products again. Service level performance was at parity with the competition. In fact most resellers claimed that their experience with the brand and the product was better than they expected. New product introductions in the second quarter of 2003 met with critical acclaim in tests, but the IT reseller channel remained unconvinced and sales were below forecast. While there were no conclusive reasons for the fall off in sales, there were no factors identifiable as providing a competitive edge. Research suggested that the reason why partners were not repurchasing the firm's products for resale was lack of customer demand. Trade promotions were introduced alongside additional demand-generation campaigns and business turned up slightly, and then downward.

In 2003 the firm augmented its usual satisfaction surveys with research into the relational exchange elements of the partnership. The results were not positive. Collaboration was low. Trust and commitment were poor compared to the competition. There was significant conflict and a lack of common goals. The causes of this poor performance were found in the quotations from the respondents:

'I started out feeling good about the firm and trained my sales guys. And then they go out and recruit my competitor.'
'The firm had a great value proposition. But all I see from them now is a series of tactical ploys that are available to everyone.'
'I had this deal, and then it went to one of their franchisees. Worse than that, he undercut me on price so much that the customer phoned me up.'

The original strategy had lost track and the actions the firm had taken for the benefit of the business were actually hurting the IT partners. An analysis of the attributes of the relationship also showed that the firm was underperforming on many important areas, and that in the last six to nine months it had lost the commitment of the partners who no longer seemed to trust the firm's intentions.

The firm recognized that it needed to resurrect the commitment and trust that it had initially been able to establish. The country managers were enlisted and a series of regional reseller forums established that provided a platform for the firm to set out a major strategic initiative for selected partners, which it backed up with a 'white paper' demonstrating its capability and competence. These forums and a European meeting of top 250 resellers, hosted by the European president, where channel strategy was shared and evidence of success presented, also gave a chance for feedback to be taken directly from the partners.

It was clear that the firm's tactical actions had diminished how the partners viewed the strategic vision of the firm. All resellers were visited by the country channel director; the visit was framed as a 'business planning' session and the account managers followed up with additional scheduled joint planning activities. These sessions helped to get the firm back into strategic planning and back onto the management agenda within the partners.

To further build on this, senior management were assigned 10 of the top resellers in each country as an internal sponsor or 'godfather' with whom serious concerns could be raised. The 'godfathers' were charged with at least one phone call per month and at least one visit per quarter to the assigned partners. The remuneration of the account managers was also changed. In addition to a quarter revenue target, various behavioural incentives were put in place including partner retention, breadth of portfolio sold by a partner and frequency of purchase. At the same time frequent and consistent joint planning became metrics of a sales rep's performance.

Channel conflict between the independent and franchised channel was inevitable, but it was realized that having the two channels reporting to two separate managers at a country and European level was fuelling the conflict. The channel organization was therefore changed so that a single executive managed both SMB channels.

The channel extranet was re-launched to ensure that IT resellers were fully aware of the information that was being provided and the support that was available. This meant that the account managers were able to free up some of their problem-solving activities and get more involved with business development. To support this, all sales reps underwent training in strategic sales and business development skills and were retrained on business management.

Managing partnership value

The concept of value in a business partnership could turn out to be extremely difficult to pin down. This is because it will consist of any number of different elements including the bottom line, top line, tangible and intangible costs and benefits. A challenge for many partnership managers is the recognition that the value drivers for their business are probably significantly different from the value drivers of their partner's business. However, when speaking to senior alliance managers they usually sum up the value of their relationship in a simple, subjective statement, for example, 'This relationship is good for us both, it works well and we intend to make it last,' or there is a simple recognition that, 'We couldn't achieve our plans without working with this firm.' It is important that any research or analysis of the elements of relationships that support these statements moves beyond subjective assessments to consider the tangible outputs that are impacted by the quality of the relationship.

Firms that enter into a buyer-seller relationship, supply chain partnership, services marketing arrangement or any other alliance formation must, by working together, use their specialized resources innovatively to achieve effective operations in line with their joint strategies. The productivity gains that can then be generated in the value chain will be above average and 'collaborative advantage' will be achieved. Moreover, this position can often lead to the development of techniques, structures, skills and processes that offer even more successful ways to cooperate and new opportunities for co-operation. These are the ultimate objectives of collaboration. Successful collaboration is highly dependent on close management and frequent, objective communication. Management must ensure that performance measures are transparent. They must create the conditions for problems to be resolved constructively and for the partnership to adapt quickly to changing situations. Investments made in the relationship by both parties underpin, reaffirm and enable the accomplishment of common goals, which spurs on the intensity of collaboration. Interpersonal relationships are enhanced and the partners become more convinced of the long-term benefits of the partnership, which reinforces the crucial value-enabling behaviours.

There is a significant gap in the level of effectiveness and efficiency of a partnership that is directly associated with the quality of the relationship management in terms of trust and commitment, mutuality of interest and collaboration. Firms should therefore consider the evaluation of these 'softer' measures within their balanced scorecards or operational metrics.

Building relationship management capabilities

In this chapter a number of key partnership dynamics have been reviewed and the importance of trust and commitment, collaboration, long-term orientation, interdependence, power, conflict, flexibility and communication highlighted. The focus has not only been on understanding and gauging the success of alliances but also the importance of being able to positively influence the value that can be achieved in a collaborative business relationship. From this discussion, Table 4.1 summarizes a number of management measures that can be taken to improve and sustain a business partnership.

However, important culture changes are also required within firms and these may not be so clear-cut or easy to implement. There is a need to develop a management philosophy or corporate ideology that values partnerships and where companies can operate in a climate of trust and openness. Corporate change of any kind is fraught with difficulties. Anecdotally the most successful partners are those firms that are forced together through adversity. The need to collaborate to survive and prosper drives many negative behaviours to extinction. This is not to say that organizational structure change or reward and remuneration changes are not also important in this regard, and high on the list is the need for senior management leadership and guidance. In this respect achieving the benefits of high performance requires a similar approach and methodology to other change programmes and initiatives.

Our research suggests that these benefits can be achieved within relatively short timescales. For example, one major firm has been able to improve its 'partner of choice' rating with its intermediaries through dedicated RM initiatives within 18 months, and has enjoyed a related greater 'share of wallet' and higher marketing investment returns.

Table 4.1 The three generations of partnering excellence

Generation	Milestones
First-generation partnering	Agreeing mutual objectives Making decisions and resolving problems openly as agreed at the start of the project Aiming at targets that provide continuous measurable improvements
Second-generation partnering	Develop strategy jointly Embrace participating firms fully Ensure equity by allowing all to be rewarded on the basis of fair prices and profits Integrate firms through cooperation and trust Benchmark performance accurately Establish best practice processes and procedures React to feedback positively and quickly
Third-generation partnering	Understand the client's business and its success factors Take joint responsibility for key outputs Turn the main processes into a seamless chain of value-adding activities Mobilize full partnership development expertise Create expert teams and key account managers Innovate jointly

Summary

This chapter has described the conditions that led firms to rediscover the importance of close customer and partner relationships but, most important, to focus their alliance objectives on their customers.

The term that describes this branch of management is 'relationship marketing'. This enlightenment reinforced the discussion on how close working partnerships could be effectively engineered and the role of power and influence. The importance of a range of partnership behaviours and, in particular, trust and commitment, were mentioned as precursors to effective teamwork. These important RM factors have been shown to be used to measure and understand a partnership such that its performance could be improved and greater value could be created. This chapter has shown that the harder, economic partnership management motives can be merged with those of RM to provide a more balanced and ultimately more productive combination.

The next chapter delves more deeply into those dynamics that can be called the 'drivers' of partnership performance, those key features that provide measures of overall value. It shows how it is possible to use these to examine substantial collaborative relationships, to derive performance metrics, and to provide diagnostics that can help managers to implement constructive change.

Key action points

1. How pervasive or 'embedded' is relationship marketing in your organization?

2. Does RM accountability reside in one place (ie, marketing) or is it more a way of doing business?

3. To what extent has your firm broadened the concept of the 'customer franchise' beyond the boundaries of the firm?

4. How would you rate your performance in terms of the level of trust or confidence that your partners have in you to 'walk the talk', manage conflict or operate common goals?

5. Looking at your partnership(s), what generation of partnering have you achieved?

5 Understanding partnership and alliance dynamics

There is an amazing lack of awareness of the wider supply/demand network.

(Professor Martin Christopher)

Introduction

Some 30 years ago classical economics took a radical step beyond the then-prevalent 'pure market forces' view of business relationship dynamics. Rather than people within business organizations simply playing a part as 'economic actors', their influence as individuals was recognized for the first time. These individuals exhibited human behaviours (idiosyncrasies, personalities and preferences) that weren't always perfect and could thus disrupt the logical flow of the business and incur additional costs. To minimize these costs and to reduce the uncertainty of such 'rogue' elements they needed to be managed. The extra costs of management and governance to cover these human risks thus had to be factored into business decision making. Many schools of thought, including organizational development strategy, the resource-based view of the firm, information and knowledge processing, organizational learning, social exchange, game theory and strategic alliances have developed alternative (and usually more complicated) theories to understand relationships between organizations. Nevertheless, this basic 'new economic' view of human behaviour within the close confines of contractual relationships has stood the test of time as a useful 'window' on the dynamics of collaborative business relationships.

This chapter first explains the key ideas behind this unusual concept of business relationship dynamics and highlights its distinctive view of organization management and human behaviour. Attempting to understand what is happening and why within complex, collaborative business partnerships is widely considered to be extremely difficult. It is shown how a simple, integrated model that uses these 'new economic' ideas creates a powerful means of objectively measuring alliance performance and understanding the underlying dynamics at play – not just what's happening but why. This model provides an important building block in our ability to specify the generic G+H Partnership Types that are described in Chapter 7. To conclude this chapter, two case studies are provided that illustrate how the partnership performance measurement technique provided organizations and their senior managers with unique and useful views that enabled them to change their businesses for the better.

A 'new economic' view of partnerships

Oliver Williamson developed his ground-breaking ideas on the human costs within business relationships in the early 1970s. Rather than supply and demand being the main drivers of business strategy, he proposed that the investment appraisal was key to deciding, for instance, whether a firm should make a product itself, team with a partner to make the product, or whether it should buy the commodity on the open market. The fundamental change from the standard practice was to factor in the overhead costs of risk management as well as the direct costs of production or acquisition. Williamson assumed from the start that all firms and individuals were self-interested, prone to taking unfair advantage or acting deviously and therefore bore an inherent risk of untrustworthiness. There were four specific human factors that he was concerned with:

1. Opportunism is taking self-centred action regardless of the impact on your partner.

2. Information impactedness is the deliberate withholding of important information, being economical with the truth or misleading your partner.

3. Uncertainty/complexity provides the opportunity to limit your commitment and to take a short-term view, especially of investment in the relationship.

4. Bounded rationality is the temptation to reduce your objectives to the 'just good enough'. This is particularly likely when pressure is high due to work and markets.

At least within one's own company it was possible to control this risk – at a cost. With external partners, this was much more risky and considerably more costly, and usually depended on contracts that were notoriously difficult to write and enforce. The latter point is well illustrated by the problems of doing business globally and needing to deal with financial, cultural, legal and time differences and language barriers.

Nevertheless, as has been shown in previous chapters, there are enormous commercial benefits to be derived from forming alliances with other firms. There is a very real possibility of combining resources and creating unique market opportunities that the firms could not achieve individually. Williamson realized that when companies formed close relationships in today's volatile, global business environment, the use of tight contracts and rules and regulations to overcome human costs was inappropriate because it reduced flexibility and innovation. Instead, as mentioned in Chapter 3, the partners jointly invest in their relationship. By providing specific, unrecoverable contributions such as information systems, training and personnel, they not only improve the efficiency of the relationship in meeting its objectives but also signal to each other their commitment, trust and willingness to cooperate. The investments also represent a form of 'bond' that increases the interdependence of the parties and dissuades them from acting selfishly (opportunistically) and thus jeopardizing the partnership (and the 'bond').

Before moving on it is worth briefly mentioning trust, although it will be considered in more detail in a later chapter. Normally trust is accepted as an essential element of successful partnerships and it tends to grow as relationships evolve through communication and experience. It is said to have substantial benefits. The parties are more willing to adapt to unanticipated problems, it reduces the risk of opportunistic behaviour, increases forbearance (patience), reduces the likelihood of information impactedness and conflict, and persuades the partners to take a longer-term view during periods of uncertainty and complexity. The 'new economic' view was not very sympathetic to these idealistic ideas. Williamson considered that in practice the temptations of opportunism made the attainment of trusting relationships a 'utopian dream' and that 'the only reliable human motive was avarice'! Instead he believed that a farsighted, calculative approach to commercial contracting was required that relied on cost-effective contractual safeguards rather than trust. Furthermore, efficiency and credibility, including reputation, were based upon 'calculativeness' where failures to perform/reciprocate were not forgotten or forgiven and would result in sanctions if they persisted. The business world was really organized in favour of 'cynics, not innocents'. Although many people today will consider this perspective overly harsh, it still retains a following in the harder schools of pragmatic management.

This section describes the interlocking elements of human behaviour that are the dynamics affecting the costs of managing an alliance relationship. It is clear that a change in one area, for example investment, will have a knock-on effect on other areas that affect relationship performance. In the next section it will be shown how this phenomenon resolves itself into two models of partnership dynamics and later it will be demonstrated how these are used to develop measures of alliance performance.

Partnerships as spiral dynamics

Always look on the bright side of life.

(Eric Idle, *Monty Python's Life of Brian*, 1979)

Let us return to our starting position in this chapter: the cost-incurring human behaviours within business relationships that need to be minimized by management and governance. Essentially, unless firms resort to harsh contractual terms and conditions and tough control procedures there is a natural tendency for engagements with other firms to become inefficient and unproductive. Ultimately the cost of managing the risks associated with human factors will either force the relationship to be dissolved and alternative sources of supply found, or if the cost and disruption make this too costly, then a sustained low performing, poor quality relationship will result. These negative dynamics are interesting because the close proximity that a partnership brings to its participants naturally involves the requirement to accommodate their needs and the acceptance of a limitation of one's own options. The rawness at the edge of business can bring to the fore Williamson's predispositions of opportunism, information impactedness, uncertainty/complexity and bounded rationality. This situation can be represented in the negative feedback loop or 'failure spiral' shown in Figure 5.1.

The uncertainty of dealing with a partner forces firms to focus on their own objectives and look to take advantage of any weakness or opportunity to improve their position, or risk being taken advantage of themselves. Experience and knowledge limitations together with fear of the unknown will persuade managers to keep those practices and processes with which they are most familiar. This translates into a firm doing as little as possible to adapt to changed conditions, and often very little to modify their process to accommodate the partner's world. At the same time, this makes firms more risk-averse and they will tend to take short-term gains rather than risk longer-term uncertainty and with it create more risk. Firms are therefore minded to reduce levels of investment in the partnership and to look for measures of immediate results rather than in process measures.

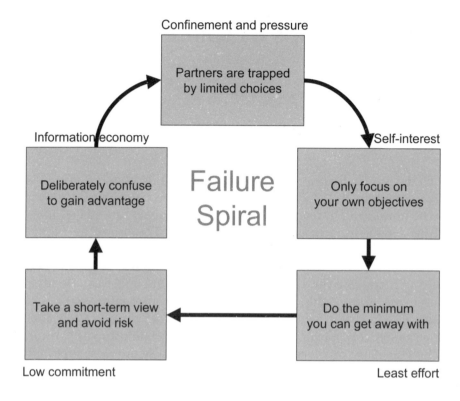

Figure 5.1 Partnership relationship failure spiral

All of this represents the management complication and cost that is endemic in business relationships with a cost-driven attitude.

The failure spiral shows the relationship dynamics that occur when negative behaviours are considered in their worst light. It is, of course, possible to use one's experience to visualize the opposite influences that might be found in a highly successful, collaborative relationship. These positive 'forces' can be viewed as the self-reinforcing, positive feedback loop or 'success spiral' shown in Figure 5.2.

In this case the business case for the partnership is strong and the parties are enthusiastic about achieving their joint aims. They concentrate on getting the product and its delivery right, which prompts staff to look for innovation in both the offering and its production. The firms feel optimistic and invest in the relationship by adding further resources and know-how. Communication at all levels begins

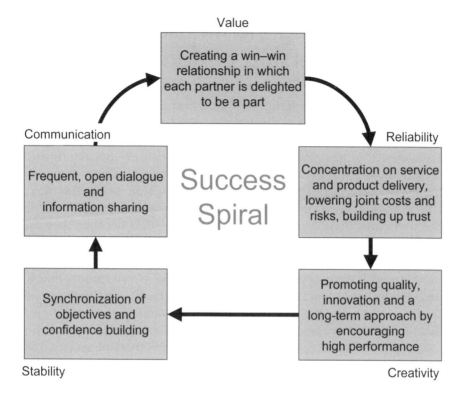

Figure 5.2 Partnership relationship success cycle

to develop and the partners believe that they have 'backed a winner'. In consequence, renewed efforts are devoted to the joint operation... and so on. It is critical to recollect that it is these high-performing relationships that are spurring above average returns and creating competitive advantage. These actions are not being undertaken in a 'humanitarian' self-indulgent manner. The firms involved recognize the gains that they can achieve and similarly recognize that a paradigm change is needed to manage the opportunity. Some might consider this utopian and unattainable, if it weren't for numerous examples, such as Coca-Cola and McDonalds, highlighted by Richard Wilding, and those in marketing channels noted by the late Professor Erin Anderson.

Finding the measure of partnership performance

Current methods of judging the value and performance of a partnership generally address the traditional time, cost and quality perspectives. They include scorecard approaches, quality systems, risk assessments, project plans, value chain analyses and financial devices such as balance sheets and investment appraisals. These focus on highly detailed aspects and often use historical, subjective data. Unfortunately, methods that take in the full gamut of relationship dynamics and their underlying causes are missing because they are generally considered to be too difficult to construct and deliver. However, performance spirals tap the key components of partnership success and failure and if metrics are applied, it will be possible to understand where improvements should be made. Furthermore, if this is used to direct the right questions to managers, the detailed diagnostics that are needed to implement change will be revealed.

In reality, alliance managers will report a spectrum of success and failure dynamics that span their commercial relationships. We have identified five relationship performance measures that evaluate the bias or tendency towards the spiral of success or the spiral of failure; these are shown in Figure 5.3.

Next, each of the key relationship performance measures are described together with the sorts of questions put to managers to assess their views from which metrics can be generated.

1. Equality

The limitations on freedom and choice a collaborative relationship entails can engender feelings of confinement and pressure. This is a 'win-lose' philosophy; firms struggle to overcome their natural reticence to discuss mutual opportunities and contributions. This can be overturned by incentivizing a quality relationship where the gains are both shared and highly rewarding. Successful negotiations can be identified where firms have explored, detailed and documented their respective cost and profit models, thereby facilitating discussions and enabling creative solutions to be agreed. In a win–win environment

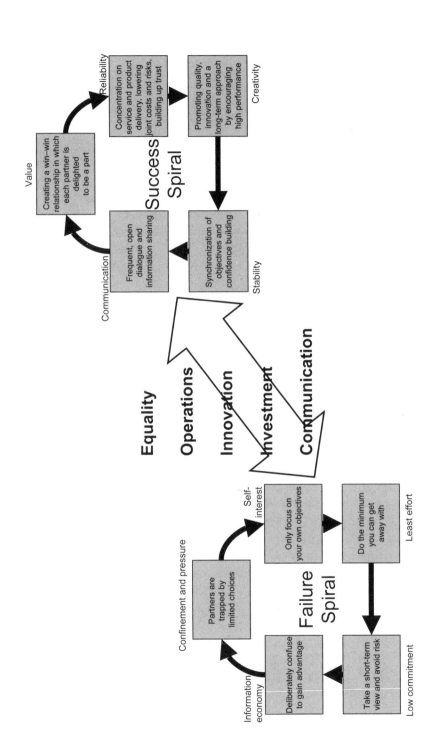

Figure 5.3 Measuring the spiral performance spectrum

the partners feel empowered to strive dynamically for the mutual good and, above all, true equity in the relationship will overcome any power imbalance. The essence is creating a win–win relationship in which each side is delighted to be a part, which can be evaluated against the following criteria:

- The gains from this relationship are equally shared between both parties.
- We do not feel imprisoned within the current relationship.
- We are willing to invest more, ie money, time, information and effort, in the current relationship.
- We are happy that our future is bound to the success of our relationship partner.
- We feel totally committed to this relationship.
- The other party is genuinely concerned that our business succeeds.
- Both sides are working to improve this relationship.

2. Operations

On the failure side, opportunism is where a firm unscrupulously seeks to serve its self-interest at the expense of its partner. It is a damaging tendency but can be reversed by strengthening the relationship through creating a more reliable business infrastructure. A focus on the quality of the relationship outputs including operational efficiency is key, as is clarity over the boundaries of the relationship. A creative approach to conflict and problem solving helps to sustain impetus. Finally, the development of goodwill, trust and commitment by incrementally building on achievements through resource commitments creates a virtuous circle. Thus the emphasis here is concentrating on service and product delivery, lowering joint costs and risks and building up trust:

- The quality of the contract outputs, ie spares, repairs and services, is entirely satisfactory.
- The quality of service delivery, ie delivery times, billing and payment, is entirely satisfactory.

- The relationship is characterized by a continually improving quality ethos.

- Problems are solved in a joint, open, constructive manner.

- Such is the goodwill in the relationship, the other party would willingly put himself out to adapt to our changing requirements.

- We trust the other party to act in our best interests.

- The responsibility for making sure the relationship works is shared jointly.

- The other party provides us with useful cost reduction and quality improvement ideas.

- The other party is always totally open and honest with us.

- The other party always does what he says he will do.

3. Innovation

Bounded rationality is the concept that individuals are rational and logical beings, but only up to a certain point. At this point rational actions are overtaken by emotional and conditional behaviours as well as by their limited information processing and communication ability. These behaviours can lead to irrational or illogical decisions, particularly in situations of pressure. The negative influence can be reversed by enabling mutual creativity through approaches such as open contracts, joint innovation, applying stretch targets, focusing on quality, ensuring disputes are resolved quickly and fairly, and by taking a long-term view of the relationship. This is the 'spark' that generates the enthusiasm to innovate and go the 'extra mile':

- The relationship encourages the achievement of high performance by both parties, ie on-time delivery and good forecasts.

- The relationship encourages us to be innovative in the way we do business.

- Performance measurement is used to raise standards.

- Disputes and problems are resolved quickly.

- Disputes and problems are resolved fairly.

- The other party is reliable and consistent in dealing with us.

- The other party is dedicated to making our business a success.

- When an unexpected problem arises, both parties would rather work out a solution than hold each other to the original contract terms.

4. Investment

Uncertainty and complexity factors have an unsettling effect on the attitudes of partners. The main consequence of environmental uncertainty is adapting to changing circumstances and overcoming the associated inertia and the costs. For example, a manufacturer which, because of competitive entry, must modify the design of its product, also may need to modify the design of the purchased components that constitute the end product. Unless a comprehensive contract can be written with its supplier that specifies in advance the required component designs and the associated terms of trade, the manufacturer may be involved in ongoing, costly negotiations that undermine its efforts to progress in the new market. This negative behaviour is usually compounded by the problem of discovering if your partner has done what he has said he will do. For example, a manufacturer may have difficulty discovering whether a distributor is providing customers with necessary pre-sales services. Even if the relevant aspects of a distributor's operations can be measured, the information gathering and processing costs incurred by the manufacturer may be substantial.

In a partnership, where there is 'strength in numbers', by achieving relationship stability and creating a framework for successful business it is possible to construct a very effective shelter against uncertainty. This involves working more closely with fewer partners and pursuing mutual objectives through value creation, joint investment and harmonized processes. It is necessary to actively manage the relationship interface through proactive relationship management, to use innovative procurement processes and, through co-operative behaviour, build interdependence between the partners. By synchronizing objectives and investing in people, processes and infrastructure, the foundations of a successful relationship can be established:

- The other party displays a sound, strategic understanding of our business.
- The objectives of both parties are clearly stated.
- The objectives of both parties are fully compatible.
- Both parties cooperate wholeheartedly.
- The relationship provides a dynamic business environment within which both parties can seek increasing rewards.
- I have complete confidence in the intentions of the other party.

5. Communication

Information impactedness is where one party has access to partnership-related information and knowledge that cannot be acquired by the other party without considerable cost and effort, and will use it to its own rather than joint advantage. This situation might occur because of greed or mistrust and will seriously hinder the efficient management and growth of an alliance. The potential consequences can be defeated by creating a communication environment optimized for success. This involves implementing multiple communication links at all levels between firms, including systematic relationship management, IS, sharing business and design data, objective performance measurement, transparency in jointly managing risk, and responding quickly to the needs of your partner. This is not just about communication frequency and quality: it also involves creating an open environment where 'cheating' will be dissuaded because of the difficulty of concealing it:

- Where the other party has proprietary information that could improve the performance of the joint business, it is freely available.
- We would welcome a shared data environment where planning, technical and pricing information is made freely available.
- We understand the information requirements of all participants in the support chain, from sub-contractors to end-user.

● Exchange of information in this relationship takes place frequently and informally, not just according to specified agreement.

● Objective performance measurement is an important part of this relationship.

● We are aware of the performance requirements for all participants in the support chain, from sub-contractors to end-user.

● We provide the other party with regular information including long-range forecasts to enable him to do his business better.

In the next sections two case studies are provided to illustrate how the approach to understanding partnering relationships can be used to assist managers to make sense of considerable complexity in order to focus their efforts on effective business improvement. The first case study demonstrates the power of our approach to understanding partnership dynamics by providing a strategic performance overview of a large number of major commercial relationships within the public sector.

UK defence relationships portfolio

In 2000 the UK defence weapons systems support teams and their collaborative industrial partners had been working for three years to improve the efficiency of their collaborative relationships under a programme called 'Smart acquisition'. A key part of this initiative was to establish joint working within integrated project teams. These organizations ensured that the Navy, Army and Air Force front-line units' weapons and equipment (ships, tanks, aircraft, etc) were properly supported with spare parts, repairs and modifications. These relationships between the UK Ministry of Defence and the world's major defence companies were strategically important because they maintained and enhanced national defence capability and, moreover, they involved a considerable expenditure of public money – nearly £12 billion in 2001.

Figure 5.4 UK defence procurement performance overview

In the past there was a long-held perception by government that these relationships did not give best value for money and adversarial and opportunistic practices were the cause. Some high-profile failures such as the tanks and rifles that were vulnerable to sand-clogging during the first Gulf War, underlined the political and public concerns for the defence equipment business. From the industry perspective, this was a hugely costly and risky business with returns taking many years to materialize. The problems were exacerbated by a customer that did not really understand the technology, frequently changed its mind and distrusted the suppliers' profit motives.

An 11-month study of 54 of these relationships using our success and failure spiral key performance measures generated the overview portrayed in Figure 5.4.

At either end of the spectrum there were the positive and negative, attracting influences that drove the relationship dynamics. The supply chain success and failure cycles are shown under 'behaviours'. The relationship performance scores are based on the statistical evaluation of managers' perceptions.

1. Equality

Equality was the best area with a rating of 68 per cent: despite many pervasive cultural problems, managers were nonetheless driven by strong desires for joint performance improvement and greater equality. They jointly realized that within a limited defence equipment market, regardless of the 'relationship atmosphere', the only option was to persevere optimistically because 'divorce' was not an option. Commitment was therefore generally strong.

2. Operations

The performance rating of only 58 per cent for operations and especially service delivery shows that it was the worst performing aspect. This was caused largely by environmental difficulties such as old technologies, high business risks and insufficient investment in IT, which made SCM hard to implement. For example, one firm offered to locate a computer terminal in the customer's organization so that orders could be placed online, but the customer's security department refused to allow it. Frustration caused by this type of behaviour resulted in opportunistic behaviour and a lack of trust and cooperation.

3. Innovation

The performance rating for innovation was 66 per cent. There was no doubt that many of the relationships in the portfolio were very proud of their technical achievements and especially their willingness to solve difficult problems at short notice. This had been proven often when unforeseen equipment failures were encountered or when severe gaps in capability as a result of contact with enemy forces were revealed. However, the impetus to devote the same enthusiasm and creativity to relationship-building was rarely present.

4. Investment

The performance rating for investment was 59 per cent. Opportunistic, short-termist behaviour such as confusing 'cheapest' for 'value for money' and a lack of flexibility over pricing reduced joint confidence in several partnerships. In one, it took the customer over a year to get a price from the supplier and then it was three times higher than the original price paid. On the other hand, customers generally fell victim to their traditional, cultural views of their suppliers by believing the suppliers were out to 'fleece' them. Nonetheless, the need for clear, joint objectives and co-operation as a means of reducing costly contract management measures were recognized by both sides in many instances.

5. Communication

The communication performance rating was 66 per cent. Problems of disclosure and the implied power balance over proprietary information were clearly evident, especially where the customer felt that it had paid for the design even though it was owned by the supplier. Failure to agree over joint performance measurement and reticence over the extent to which this should be transparent often reduced cooperative performance to very low levels. Nevertheless, free, frequent information sharing and considerable relationship investments such as shared data environments were also evident in some relationships.

The main specific issues that emerged in this case were as follows.

Financial

Annually set, fixed budgets and government accounting systems were not designed to cope with new, relational, framework contracts. These caused both customer and supplier teams severe management difficulties and tended to undermine the 'Smart acquisition' ethos. On the other hand, the lack of stable customer funding arrangements due to politically-motivated budget fluctuations prevented suppliers from carrying out effective investment planning, which generated other long-term costs that were inevitably passed on to the customer:

'Our fear is the feast and famine situation of defence spending. There are times when we must stop work, lay off experienced staff and then race to get back going again. I worry that we cannot respond fast enough and this adversely affects our service to the end-customer.'
'Budget constraints in the Ministry of Defence reduce the relationship to fire-fighting. It's impossible for us to plan ahead.'

'We are about to sign an incentivized contract and if he (the contractor) does well he will get paid more, but I have not got the extra money in my budget. Smart acquisition is not geared up for this kind of flexibility.'

Commercial

A variety of governance types were in use, from very flexible, long-term, incentivized performance framework contracts to highly detailed, prescriptive arrangements containing penalty clauses for poor performance. The older relationships were generally based upon regulation (tightly worded contracts) and although some were successful the majority were not, and team leaders were loath to adopt long-term, more flexible contracts until they could trust the other party to deliver an efficient service. This was actually a self-defeating (failure spiral) decision because a dominant reason for problems was the inability of these relationships to adapt to changing circumstances. Staff were very enthusiastic about the newer, relational, long-term contracts because they contained innovative features that incentivized performance and provided overt benefit-sharing. But in one case where the arrangement had been in place for five years, considerable problems were being encountered (including a loss of trust) in trying to adjust to unforeseen environmental turbulence. Adversarial, bureaucratic commercial practices and attitudes still existed in both the MoD and the defence industries' cultures. These often increased project costs, caused delays and reduced trust:

'The biggest obstacle to improving business performance is the commercial department. There is a severe shortage of resources, risk aversion and lack of flexibility, which leads to significant effort and delay in agreeing contracts.'

'A major success factor was the unusual combination of commercial staff on both sides who were lateral thinking and open to new ways of doing business.'

'They have an air of arrogance – "take it or leave it, we are the sole supplier".'

'We have built a "head" of goodwill to make this contract work despite the traditional problems that won't go away.'

Staff

Operationally both sides realized the importance of personal contributions to relationship performance but corporate HR policies were generally not in tune. There was a lack of investment in good staff and a reluctance to relinquish traditional two-year assignments. In long-term, highly technical projects the unnaturally high staff turnover prevented personal relationship development and the accumulation of learning and experience, and promoted inefficient business processes. The lack of culture-matching resulting in 'them and us' attitudes was acknowledged as a long-standing problem; the need for an open, no-blame culture aimed at customer and relationship satisfaction was also acknowledged. However, little substantive effort had been made to address these fundamental issues:

'The regular cycling of staff is not conducive to building long-term relationships that develop sound working practices and innovation.'

'By having a member of staff in their team we are able to communicate much better, reduce misunderstandings, and gain a much clearer idea of the plans for the business. We did this despite our head office.'

Performance

Generally there was very poor perception of how end-to-end supply chain performance should be measured and few clear, visible performance objectives agreed by all supply chain players including the end-customers. Frequent, interactive, open communication across all levels of the customer/supplier interface, especially on performance reviews and continuous improvement of products/services and business processes, were also rare:

'There is a gulf in perception between the sides over performance, which also extends to the front line (end-customers). Without a common understanding of how we are doing and what we must achieve we cannot move forward.'

In our second case study the focus is on a pair of SMEs. Although there are many examples of the dynamics of larger alliances, there is benefit in examining the microcosm within a small business because it brings into very sharp relief a number of salient points that are generic to all partnerships.

Sonatest and Paragon

This case study describes how Sonatest NDE Group plc, an electronics manufacturer, and Paragon Electronic Components plc, a specialist components supplier, used success and failure spiral partnering key performance measures to assess their relationship quality and value. The exercise revealed that the existing supplier relationship management system had not optimized the returns from the relationship. As a result both customer and supplier were able to make substantial improvements to the bottom line. They also learnt, for the first time, how to manage a partnering relationship more effectively to secure long-term benefits.

Sonatest is based in Milton Keynes, UK, and has 150 employees and revenues of £18 million. It is an industry leader in the field of non-destructive testing equipment and uses high levels of investment in research and design to manufacture and distribute some of the world's best NDT products from six locations worldwide. Its customer base covers a range of industries including oil, rail, manufacturing and aerospace. Sonatest is characterized by an entrepreneurial, innovative, engineering culture.

Paragon is part of a group of companies providing specialist electronics supply chain management and contract electronics manufacturing services. With annual revenues of over £30 million, Paragon employs over 300 people and is acknowledged as the UK's leading company in its field. One of its key strengths is supplying companies that produce low to medium volume complex products, with all component kits supplied 'assembly ready' and tailored to individual requirements. Its services include purchasing and progressing through inspection, stock control and accounts, thus freeing up their customers' resources for more strategic activities. The focus is on precision, planning and procurement.

The 10-year relationship between these two SMEs was perceived by both CEOs as successful. However, the relationship assessment revealed untapped potential. Both companies experienced a watershed in their development thanks to rapid growth in their respective markets, so both CEOs decided to appoint new managing directors. In addition, as they planned to collaborate on a major new product development, the CEOs decided to benchmark the relationship value between their two organizations. They wanted an objective view of the effectiveness of their business collaboration and sought recommendations on how to improve joint performance. Using a series of benchmarks based on the characteristics of best-in-class collaborative relationships, this partnership revealed a number of crucial areas for improving teamwork, shown in Table 5.1.

Table 5.1 Mapping the Sonatest/Paragon relationship to best-in-class

Benchmark	Assessment
Joint innovation	Yes, but scope for improvement
Customer focus	Yes
High quality outputs	Yes, but scope for improvement
World-beating practices	Yes, but not integrated
Continuous improvement	Partially, but not integrated
Flexible commercial frameworks	Verbal agreement
Objective performance measurement	Yes, but not integrated
Improved business forecasting	Yes, but scope for improvement
Coordinated processes	Yes, but scope for improvement
Honest and open communication	Yes
Two-way information flows	Yes, but not integrated
Clear relationship management	Partially, but not integrated

The Sonatest/Paragon relationship mapped to best-in-class in just two areas: customer focus, and honest and open communication. In other areas such as joint innovation, the quality of outputs, forecasting and coordinated processes, there was room for improvement. Individually, the partners had some world-beating practices, performance measures, relationship management and formal communication, but these were not sufficiently integrated. Information flows within Sonatest, and between it and Paragon, tended to be uncoordinated. This had sometimes resulted in last-minute ordering of components, unreliable planning, forecasting and decision making, inadequate information feedback and dissemination, compartmentalization of important information, and insufficient knowledge about the partner's capabilities and limitations. As a Paragon manager commented, 'They have a bit of a gap between the engineers and other departments such as purchasing, R&D and commercial. Sometimes we, their supplier, have to bridge this gap for them.'

Another area in which value was not being maximized was clear, joint performance targets. For example, shared performance targets could have been set for component availability, test yields, customer returns and ongoing cost reductions. Their dearth tended to drive up inventory holdings, rework costs and delays, and potentially impacted on end-customer satisfaction and business profitability. A Paragon interviewee pointed out, 'They have placed orders without delivery dates or defined requirements. Better forecasts would mean everyone could be leaner.'

In addition to integrated shared targets, the third significant issue was related to process management. It was apparent that, over time, joint operational processes had become ill-defined, indicating that there was no central point of responsibility for maintaining coherence. As a consequence, individuals had developed their own practices, which created gaps and overlaps and increased costs and risks. The analysis revealed the potential for greater overall integration to increase the value generated by the relationship.

Lynette Ryals, Cranfield School of Management, has proposed that when procurement managers (PMs) are attempting a more strategic stance they need to view themselves as relationship managers (RMs). The integration between supplier and customer firms is probably one of the most difficult areas to implement, although it does have substantial value-generating potential. Shared targets are slightly easier, although they do require the PM to have a strategic vision and also to have trust in the supplier. The process management issues are well known to PMs, and providing (and enforcing) a centralized contract and set of processes is an important function. The Sonatest/Paragon relationship provides an illustration of the opportunities for value creation over and above operational improvements.

The senior managers in both companies were surprised by the results of the assessment because it revealed a number of important operating issues of which they were unaware. Although there was a clear understanding between the companies at senior level, this was not apparent at lower levels. Despite these issues, the collaboration brought both companies considerable business benefits and there was a very strong commitment by all staff in both firms to the relationship and its future success. As a Sonatest respondent pointed out, 'Of all our partners, this relationship still has magic. We probably wouldn't go anywhere else. We have a lot invested in the relationship and get a good return from it.'

The analysis not only revealed some areas where the relationship could work better at a strategic level. It also became clear that the supplier had a lot more to offer than the customer recognized; an opportunity for value creation had been missed through under-utilization of its resources and skills. It also illustrates the danger of supplier relationship management systems, if they exist. They tend to measure historic performance rather than future potential and concentrate on a lower level of detail that fails to 'tap' the health of the relationship as a whole. The second problem is that the perception of the relationship is diffused throughout the two organizations and there is often no central, joint focus for the management of the relationship.

The performance assessment allowed the companies to take an objective view of their relationship, instead of one fraught with individual opinion and fear of upsetting the status quo. A Sonatest representative commented, 'We have not resolved all our problems, but we now have a relationship that allows us to raise them, and discuss a way forward without conflict.' A quick win out of the review was a £40,000 per year saving on in-house testing within Sonatest, because it was realized that boards supplied by Paragon were already fully tested and certified.

The assessment recommended a more robust joint business framework that better supported the complexity of the relationship be put in place. The companies jointly agreed to formalize processes and to hold regular planning meetings that would also review performance, work-in-progress and sales against orders. To improve communication they decided that Paragon technical representatives would spend more time in the Sonatest factory.

As a result of the closer collaboration between the companies, a joint team working on the design of the new versions of Sonatest's leading products transformed the development process and shortened the time to market from five years to one year. As part of this, Paragon proposed a number of additional services, ie design-for-manufacture and design-for-test. These measures resulted in improved first-time manufacturing yield from around 50 per cent to over 95 per cent; the use of cheaper, more reliable components with greater functionality; and improved delivery time to end-customers from four to two weeks. Furthermore, pushing manufacturing even further back into Paragon was under active consideration so Sonatest could concentrate on its core strengths of designing new strategic products, marketing, distribution and customer service. As a Paragon participant put it, 'Together we have a new way of working that allows us to focus even more clearly on the customers.'

Enhanced interaction made the partners realize that use of aging technology and uncertain consumption information required excessive and costly stockholdings. A review resulted in more relevant holdings and the disposal of redundant items. Furthermore, improved forecasting from regular reviews of forward order book and supply chain requirements resulted in significantly better availability at lower cost. Sonatest realized that its IT systems were fragmented and not providing adequate management information. The review diagnostics enabled it to accurately define the requirements for a new IT package to be used to integrate production, stock ordering and CRM.

Over the following three years the customer's revenues rose by 38 per cent and those of the supplier by 100 per cent.

Conclusion

This chapter has shown how it is possible to identify some key relationship factors that go to the heart of the interaction between collaborative business partners. From this, positive and negative feedback loops (spirals) of behaviour can be proposed, and the views of alliance managers seen through two case studies reveals how they could be used to create objective assessments of partnership dynamics. These were of such detail that they enabled managers to target the appropriate, bottom-line areas for improvement. Given that current management performance monitoring and measurement systems still focus on traditional time, cost and quality factors with only variable success, a truly objective assessment technique for commercial relationships is indeed of revolutionary importance.

The next chapter pulls together the major streams of discussion so far to describe a model that represents partnership performance in terms of three critical bundles of behaviours and activities. From this model it is possible to consider the implications and consequences of good, poor or average demonstration and performance of these behaviours and activities such that managers have a tool against which partnerships can be assessed and compared, and corrective or remedial actions can be identified.

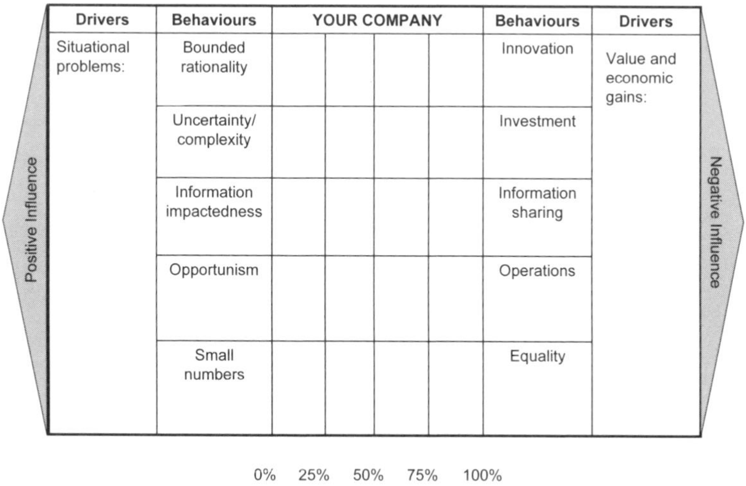

Drivers	Behaviours	YOUR COMPANY				Behaviours	Drivers
Situational problems:	Bounded rationality					Innovation	Value and economic gains:
	Uncertainty/ complexity					Investment	
	Information impactedness					Information sharing	
	Opportunism					Operations	
	Small numbers					Equality	

Positive Influence ◁ / Negative Influence ▷

0%   25%   50%   75%   100%

Figure 5.5 Partnership self-assessment

Key action points

1. Consider your most important commercial relationships in the light of the success/failure spiral key performance measures shown in Figure 5.3 on page 123.

2. For each of these relationships ask yourself the questions listed in this chapter under each key performance measure for equality, operations, innovation, investment and communications. Plot your results in Figure 5.5 and gain an impression of how well you think each is performing.

3. Better still, ask your opposite number in a partner firm the same questions and compare your responses.

4. Taking all things onto consideration, is your partnership(s) or alliance in a spiral of success or failure?

5. Using Figure 5.5, identify the extent to which your firm is exhibiting negative behaviours in the light of your partnership(s).

6. Given your assessment, what position would you foresee for the next six to nine months?

7. What would you see to be the consequences of such an improvement/decline?

6 Working hard at the 'soft' factors

It's the quality of the relationship that counts: plus the effort you put into making it work.

(Michel Clement, Vice President, Oracle, EMEA)

Introduction

So far it has been shown how managers have responded to the increasing pace of change that has affected their endeavours over the last 50 or 60 years. Many of the mechanistic approaches to improving quality and customer service have delivered considerable dividends but, in recent times, new initiatives have been needed to satisfy the market. These have largely revolved around improving teamwork in the business chain. In the past, working with competitors was not an option; after all, they were our 'deadly enemies'. Nowadays and quite counter-intuitively, firms are learning to manage a wide range of alliances simultaneously, sometimes including and sometimes against their competitors. Knowing how to manage these relationships, how to measure their performance, and how to get the best from them are crucial capabilities for future success in ever-more turbulent markets.

A number of key factors including cooperation, interdependence, commitment and trust have been identified and it has been shown that they influence alliance performance through the spirals of success and failure. This chapter will show how these key factors can be assembled into an all-embracing model that can be used to describe and assess business partnership performance. Three groupings define the way in which firms perform and demonstrate their partnership capabilities: collaborative innovation, partnership quality and value creation. The model provides a framework within which the seemingly random variations in the behaviour of partners can be consistently interpreted and understood, whether their relationships are supply chain partnerships, key accounts, marketing channels or strategic alliances. It allows characteristic relationship types to be identified based on proven parameters and, critically, offers clear tactical and strategic pointers to managers on the best way ahead. This chapter is therefore about bringing together the ideas about the partnership dynamics that affect bottom-line performance. Chapter 7 will show how this model is used to generate eight archetypal Gibbs+Humphries Partnership Types.

Evaluating partnership performance

Typically firms will consider operational excellence and its elements as major partnering objectives: product, quality, price, service, support and physical distribution. These are underpinned by a market or customer orientation and are supported by process design, management and performance measurement. The importance and intensity of partnership management cannot be overestimated and the quality of the relationship will impact not only the management cost but also the operational inputs and outputs. Thus assessing whether a relationship between a manufacturer and an intermediary can be considered successful means reviewing all aspects of the relationship, that is the total performance of the relationship to the reseller. The same is true for supply chain and strategic alliance partners: it is the overall performance that is important.

While there is a 'natural' management focus on the tangible outcomes from the partnership, there is typically less focus on what can be considered as the affective outcomes or the leading indicators. That is, the factors that influence the productivity and effectiveness, namely the quality of the 'partnering' itself.

Partnership performance is characterized by relational factors such as closeness, interdependence and the presence of an array of social norms and practices. It is also possible to consider extremes where positive relational factors contribute to high performance compared to negative relational factors that contribute to low performance. As such it is important to note that:

- Organizations can and do identify specific factors that affect relational performance in their dealings with other firms.

- Partnerships and alliances do vary in terms of their perceived performance of relational factors.

- Relational performance can have an important bearing on the commercial outcome of the relationship.

The above can be summarized in considering the quality of the relationship. However, there are a number of different ideas on what comprises this relationship quality or the 'perceived relationship performance'. These overlapping concepts include:

- trust, commitment and the absence of opportunism (selfishness) that affects the 'climate' of a relationship;

- primary partnership success factors including profitability, learning and market opportunities;

- a bundle of intangibles such as reputation and know-how that augments products and services;

- being able to achieve the added benefits that follow from prolonged social relations as found in some service providers compared to the traditional professional supplier competence relationship;

- the enhanced buyer-salesperson interaction where relationship performance results from trust and satisfaction;

- the assessment of business teamwork by senior managers in both firms of the partnership where they also compare their relationship with potential alternatives as a benchmark.

Extensive research over the last 10 years has identified the factors that generate partnering performance and culminate in partnering excellence that have as their consequence the extraordinary gains and benefits of successful business-to-business partnerships. The following three 'super' partnership success factors have been synthesized through research, which when combined, provide a comprehensive measure of alliance performance:

1. *Collaborative innovation* – the conditions that describe the effectiveness of the relationship and enable the partnership to be innovative and to respond to opportunities.

2. *Partnership quality* – the quality of the relationship exchange including commitment and trust.

3. *Value creation* – the efficiency of the partnership to create and capture the potential value that the partnership offers.

These have proved to be penetrating 'lenses' through which it is possible to explore the activities and behaviours that promote partnership success. They enable firms to determine whether they are in the spiral of decline or success. Firms are able to identify their strengths and weaknesses and to initiate corrective actions to ensure partnership success. Figure 6.1 brings these relationships and the operational factors into a unified model that represents partnership performance.

The next section describes and illustrates each of these 'super' factors by considering the opportunities and challenges that they offer.

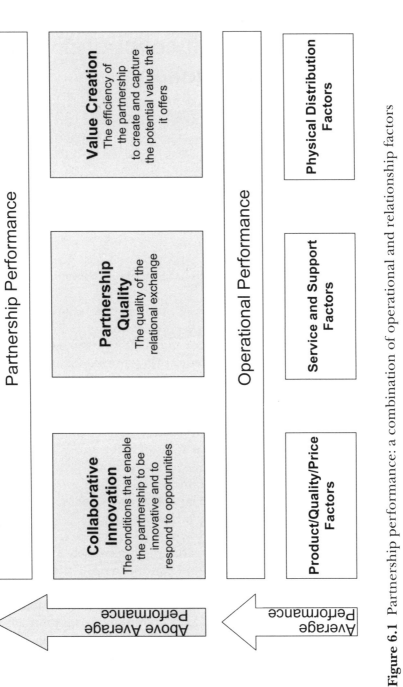

Figure 6.1 Partnership performance: a combination of operational and relationship factors

Opportunities and challenges created through collaborative innovation

Collaborative innovation concerns the actions that are promoted and encouraged as a consequence of satisfactory partnership activities such as joint working and common initiatives. It is this aspect of a good relationship that is most often thought of as a hard working partnership. This is the 'engine house' of success, but without coaxing and encouragement, partnerships often stall and fail to spark. Collaborative innovation can be thought of as the effectiveness of the relationship as it produces tangible outcomes such as share of wallet, growth and scale/frequency of joint projects and bids. Collaborative innovation enables partnerships to achieve their fundamental aims and objectives.

'Working together' or 'teamwork' is a fundamental requirement of an effective partnership and because cooperation, coordination and collaboration are closely related they can be grouped together as 'C3 behaviour'. This is working together to bring diverse resources into a required relationship to achieve effective operations in harmony with the strategies and objectives of the parties involved. The importance of pursuing mutually beneficial interests cannot be underrated but it also emphasizes the essentially cooperative nature of partnerships characterized by balance and harmony. Under these conditions positive feedback 'kicks in' and productive relationships can often lead to the discovery of even more successful ways to cooperate and new objects of cooperation. In other words, good behaviour will be reciprocated and a success spiral is possible and accelerated.

C3 behaviour can be used to achieve honed processes, structures, skills and innovation. In a product-oriented approach, buyers and sellers join together to innovate and produce competitive, quality products, and are able to contain or restrict costs for as long as possible. In the supply chain the early involvement of the supplier's expertise in the design phase will bring about significant joint benefits. C3 behaviour is thus an essential factor in contributing to the practical success of business-to-business relationships. It signifies joint endeavours to achieve common objectives and hence relationship success. It enables creative, innovative solutions to be developed that generate new value, products or processes and, in the end, create a very powerful, intangible value in the form of 'collaborative advantage'.

Another important component of collaborative innovation is the partnership's ability to adapt to changing internal and external circumstances. Products, procedures, inventory management, attitudes, values and goals may all need to change to maintain the competitiveness of the alliance. Such changes will be impacted by the type and complexity of the product/service, the depth of information exchanged and the extent of organizational social and operational contacts and degree of cooperation required. A flexible commercial framework is a sound enabler of adaptation because it gets people to concentrate on outputs and the customer rather than the 'small print'. It is a well-known truism that penalty clauses never create customer satisfaction.

Communication follows on from and is a requirement of a successful working partnership and thus follows the behaviour spirals model. It is in many ways the enabler for all collaborative innovation activities. It contains honest, open channels for joint planning and goal setting where mutual expectations are established and measured and allows the breadth and depth of the complex interaction to be managed. At the operational level, clear guidelines on the sharing of proprietary information and technology positively influence product development, costs, sales and revenues. They also increase commitment and trust. Overall, the degree of transparency achieved in a partnership or alliance will inevitably set the scene for success. Table 6.1 shows a summary of the main components of partnership quality.

Table 6.1 The main components of collaborative innovation

Adaptability	Innovation	Communication	Cooperation
Ability of the partnership to adapt to changing conditions	Extent to which the partnership encourages innovation and high performance	Quality, relevance, timeliness and openness of communication	Extent to which the partners cooperate effectively
The capability of the partnership to maintain and improve its competitive position through process improvements and cost initiatives		The ability of the partnership to coordinate and execute their teamwork to achieve agreed objectives	

IT distribution

Mergers and acquisitions within the IT sector, like many others, are frequent and usually traumatic. In this case study a distribution and logistics organization in Spain was acquired by a larger multi-country distributor organization headquartered outside of Spain. The Spanish distributor had been a major route to market for a global manufacturer and the risk was high that resellers would desert the new owner and move their business to another distributor firm. There was also a risk that resellers would desert the manufacturer and switch to other competitive brands as the erstwhile organization had a high reputation for value-added services while the new owner had a greater focus on speed and efficiency with no frills. For the new owners the downside was the risk that the manufacturer would look to reduce the importance of the franchise and divert sales to a second and third distributor already in place in Spain.

Following a series of reviews that helped to iron out the ongoing commercial context of the partnership, the firms involved framed the problem statement in terms of the retention, expansion and satisfaction of the existing reseller base. This was set against a backdrop of the new owner expressing its intention to radically overhaul existing IT systems and critical processes with a view to drive down 'unnecessary' costs and increase inventory turnover. Both firms recognized the desirability of the continuation of the business partnership but had concerns over the viability of the seemingly contrasting operational needs of the resellers, the leaner strategy proposed by the distributor, and the prerequisites of the manufacturer's products.

The two firms set up a series of workshops to review the implications of the new organization on the reseller community. A series of formalized information exchanges took place that detailed the products, their configuration needs, and the supply chain dynamics together with the infrastructure changes that were being proposed within the distributor.

Dedicated change management procedures were put in place to galvanize the teams and to ensure a focus on the medium and longer-term objectives of the transition. The change management team also made sure that the resellers were recognized as key stakeholders and brought into the discussions as appropriate. This engagement of the resellers identified their requirements in terms of critical business enablers such as credit availability, configuration services and returns policies. Information flow was critical to all partners and a dedicated web bulletin board was set up enabling the project's activities and plan to be reviewed and to act as a central repository for data and information.

A key investment by both parties was the establishment of electronic data interfaces (EDI) linkages, which enable electronic order processing and invoicing. This also supported quicker payment of distributor claims as a consequence of any special or promotional pricing that the manufacturer initiated on products. IT investment also extended to providing real-time information on local and central inventory and shipments. The establishment of a virtual buffer stock in the distributor warehouse enabled quick turnaround on reseller orders and a greater availability of products and configurations. This was a compromise on the part of both firms, which held differing positions in terms of the level of inventory that was required to fulfil ongoing demand.

The new arrangements brought with them the need to readdress the critical success measures of the relationship. While the previous relationship had focused almost exclusively on activity (the number of units shipped), the new partnership brought with it a series of broader metrics that were reviewed and monitored against agreed benchmarks. Associated business reviews and greater leverage of data enabled the firms to improve the level of outlook accuracy, which further enhanced overall profitability and encouraged the firms to launch a series of successful reseller recruitment programmes.

Typical symptoms of ineffective collaborative innovation

To understand the benefits of collaborative innovation it is appropriate to consider some typical situations where it is obviously not working. These mainly concern the management of operations:

- Responsibilities are shirked.

- Information is not shared effectively.

- Pockets of understanding – the 'inner circle' mentality.

- 'Intellectual snooping' – information is informally collected by a partner.

- Focus is on the product rather than the solution for the customer.

- Account managers become 'problem solvers' or 'query managers'.

- Large numbers of transactional, low value or infrequent selling cycles.

- Basic process disconnects, eg internal processes are used to manage external partners.

- Lack of proactivity with over-reliance on the host to initiate activities and come up with ideas.

- Customers are 'mis-sold' products.

- There is a lack of strategic selling skills, which results in product-benefits being dominant in marketing and sales activities.

- Falling customer satisfaction as the appropriate behaviours are not displayed by a partner.

- Recruitment of partners is difficult.

- Dedicated partner managers have multiple conflicting account-abilities.

- Planning workshops are dominated by business reviews.

- Joint planning sessions are task/target cascades.

Opportunities and challenges created through partnership quality

Partnership quality is the second key driver of the overall success of a commercial relationship. It forms the basis upon which partnership productivity takes place. Partnership quality is not simply a passive contributor to alliances but directly influences important factors such as the duration and longevity of the relationship itself. This 'super' factor is also associated with overall satisfaction and forms a hard link between the operational performance of the business and the effective evaluation of partnership success. Partnership quality is also directly associated with a firm's ability to capture the value that is created through an effective partnership, that is to take the gains and benefits to the bottom or top line of the P&L.

It is significant that partnership quality will develop over time and is an important factor in the founding and early stages of the partnership. The trust and commitment in an alliance or other business-to-business relationship very much depends on mutual perceptions and sometimes it takes one or other of the partners to make the first move. Usually through a series of initially small projects or demonstrations of commitment, the partners learn to trust each other and as a result are willing to commit more resources to the relationship. A positive spiral of behaviour and growing commitment begins with continuously improving results if the effort is maintained by both sides. In a channels context these investments can be in the form of training provided by the host firm as well as accreditation gained or earned by the partner. In strategic alliances investment can take the form of the provision of facilities, people and know-how. These positive behaviours significantly reduce reliance on the contract to 'keep the peace' and once people begin working together and understanding what they have to do to create joint value, selfish behaviour and its management costs reduce significantly. The resultant increase in partnership quality frees up management resources to develop and optimize the business. They can also feel confident in taking a long-term view as opposed to constantly watching out for faults in the other side.

Partnership quality can also be initiated because a firm has a good reputation within the market and the industry, and has established partnerships and networks. This is usually based on good practice developed through experience. Firms such as Honda and Philips have no difficulty in finding high performing partners to join their enterprises. These firms are usually very successful and known as 'a pleasure to do business with'. Such firms will value good interpersonal relationships because they foster trust. However, they will know where to 'draw the line' and will not allow their partnerships to become 'country clubs' where 'cosy' relationships are complacent, flabby and under-performing

At the other end of a partnership lifecycle, commitment can build up to significant levels. Firms generally believe themselves to be independent and free to make decisions that affect their future. Within a partnership or alliance, a point is usually reached when the parties are totally dependent on each other for the delivery of the outputs. One firm uses its unique design and manufacturing skills while the other uses its unique marketing and sales skills. They have reached the point of interdependence. For some organization cultures this may be a difficult thing to accept even though it is the only way to achieve the maximum effectiveness of the joint enterprise.

They can no longer take many decisions, for example moving a main distribution point, without first considering the needs of their partner. Thus, without careful understanding and management, it is only too easy to allow small irritations to grow in a negative feedback failure spiral and to undermine the stability of the partnership.

One way of overcoming some of the frictions associated with interdependence is to make partner development one of the aims of the joint enterprise. It is recognized that very high performing partnerships and alliances are characterized by their ability to share knowledge about processes, know-how, skills and customers. This transfer of knowledge, often through training or the setting up of joint operations, will strengthen the business and allow new resources and capabilities to be created. Table 6.2 shows a summary of the main components of partnership quality.

Table 6.2 The factors that make up partnership quality

Commitment	Trust
The motivation to invest in the maintenance and development of the partnership	The extent to which a partner(s) is believed to be trustworthy, reliable and credible
The extent to which investments are made in the partnership by both/all parties	The degree to which the partnership is operationalized in terms of mutual interests and benefits

Cereals supply chain

Two UK organizations, the Home Grown Cereals Association and the Institute of Grocery Distributors, recently sponsored a study into the effectiveness of cereals supply chains. It was felt there was a strong need to increase the industry's cohesion and to spread best practice on collaboration.

In the brewing supply chain, farmers sold their grain directly to the brewers. Analysis of these relationships revealed that although there was considerable interdependence between the sides, the brewers thought the farmers were reactionary and unwilling to cooperate. 'They sit on their farms as they always have done and take all our efforts to change the way we do business as interference.' On the other hand, the farmers felt alienated and undervalued by their partners who appeared to manage by 'dictum'. 'They visit us in smart suits and attempt to blind us with management-speak. They show no understanding of what grain production is all about.' There was little effort by either side to understand the other and as a result both trust and commitment were very low. This had an adverse effect on efficiency and returns.

In the baking supply chain, the farmers had created an intermediary organization to store and market their grain. As a result a very close relationship between the intermediary and the milling companies and the bakers had built up. The farmers gained accurate planning information and feedback to enable them to develop new strains of wheat. 'Our intermediary speaks our language and stands up for our interests with our customers. We have a very clear idea of what we need to do and we always do our best to do it.' The customers gained high quality products when they needed them and at a competitive price. Moreover, important R&D carried out by the farmers ensured they could continue to develop competitive products. 'We are all committed to satisfying customers and will move heaven and earth to be the best in the market. There is a lot of trust all round because we know that everyone is a vital link in the chain'.

Typical symptoms of ineffective partnership quality

Typical symptoms of situations where trust and commitment are not being applied effectively and are thus undermining partnership quality include:

- Partners reduce investment in the host's brand or service or in the overall relationship.

- One party is seen as a minor player in a broader network of alliances and is (often unintentionally) excluded from key events.

- Partners compete for major accounts with alternative partners.

- Partners do not make key senior or support staff available for meetings or training.

- End-customer business experience is poor.

- Relationship investments are underutilized or 'stranded'.

- New initiatives are not adopted wholeheartedly or are missed altogether.

- Relationships are typically short-lived.

- Value cannot be captured and neither the costs nor the gains can be accounted for.

- Unrealistic objectives are set and there is an expectation that high returns are possible in the short term.

- Misappropriation of partners' resources such as technology, customers and people (staff).

Opportunities and challenges of creating value

As well as adding value, value creation is a vital reason for firms to work together – being stimulated to develop something new beyond the initial reason for the partnership. The ability of firms to capture the total value – 'value realization' – in the form of benefits to the end-customers and to the firm's profitability is the ultimate objective of a partnership or alliance. Creating value can also be associated with service quality and perceived service quality. Many firms are aware of the importance of operational excellence and will focus much effort on understanding their relative standard of performance. However, while the operational satisfaction of a strategic partner remains important, a more critical set of factors needs to be considered that relate to the ability of the relationship itself to add, create and capture value and to do this consistently within a stable relationship. It has been found that operational performance satisfaction (for example with a query management system) does not automatically lead to increases in profitability or sales, but creating and capturing value can be considered as the efficiency rating of a relationship as it influences the ROMI and ROI as well as gross margin of the firms involved. Inevitably, therefore, value creation is a sum of all the relationship-building, sustaining and developing behaviours that take place. Concentration on only a sub-set, such as financial measures, is unlikely to achieve the full potential of the combined enterprise.

It is well known that too much reliance on traditional commercial elements such as product or brand is less effective in driving a successful, profitable partnership than factors such as productive synergy. Productive synergy deals with the ability of the partnership to operate effectively at high intensity. Conflict is inevitable, but conflict here is constructive because within the established boundaries of common goals, firms can use heated discussion to fuse together new ideas to create new processes, to be swift in getting to market or to out-manoeuvre competitors. Issues are always dealt with quickly and fairly to ensure that momentum is not lost by risking falling into the negative behaviour spiral. Very successful partnerships are 'reliably unstable'; that is, they utilize performance indicators to improve processes and enable new efficiencies. They are self-challenging and critical but at the same time positive and constructive in moving forward. In contrast, major institutions are often characterized as having moribund processes 'weighing and measuring each turn of the screw simply to report its weight and measure'.

Managers generally recognize that enforcing contracts through litigation is a waste of time and money and certainly not a basis for thriving partnerships. Sometimes the best contract is the one that is filed and forgotten as soon as it is inked, allowing the firms to concentrate on making the partnership work. Contracts should be drawn up in the same spirit as a pre-nuptial agreement, which is concerned with the consequence of relationship break-up and not with predefining how the relationship should work. The dynamic forces affecting virtually all partnerships render most attempts to foresee all the likely problems in a contract impractical. As such it is important that a partnership is governed within a flexible agreement that focuses the attention on the customers. It should incentivize high performance, promote a quality ethos, sustain continuous improvement and allow the equitable sharing of profits and other benefits. Given this foundation, partnerships can concentrate on achieving consistency of process supported by factual evidence rather than hearsay. This factual evidence is provided by the use of jointly defined, fully transparent performance metrics that not only embrace financial and operational activities but also the wider, relational drivers that affect overall success. Table 6.3 shows a summary of the main components of value creation.

Table 6.3 The factors that make up value creation

Conflict management	Synergy	Value creation	Process efficiency
The ability of the partnership to manage inherent conflicts	The extent to which the partners share common aims and objectives	The strength of the underlying economic proposition of the partnership	Ensuring a focus on continuous process improvement of the partnership outputs/ deliverables
The degree to which the partnership creates an environment for creative issue or problem resolution		The capacity of the partnership to consistently improve its competitive position through process improvements and cost initiatives	

The Hunter Valley Coal Chain

John Gattorna, a senior academic figure in supply chain management, has made a special study of the Hunter Valley Coal Chain (HVCC). This is a complex operation that moves almost 100 million tons of coal each year from 30 producers to customers in Japan, Korea and China. This volume is slated to steadily increase at least over the next 10 years. The business is worth US$5,355 billion per year and thus provides huge value to Australia and the businesses involved.

Considerable efforts have been made by the Logistics Team, a joint venture made up of the six main providers, to improve teamwork in the supply chain. This comprises train, track, terminal and port handling companies. By working together and using innovative planning and scheduling IT, costs have been reduced and efficient operations have been established. Moreover, a continuous improvement programme is part of the business. However, there are problems on either end of this logistics operation. The mining operators are independently-minded and can be difficult to deal with, especially in predicting production estimates of different product grades. At the other end, under rather loose contract arrangements, ships arrive at Port Waratah to be dealt with on a first-come, first-served basis with virtually no coordination with the production schedule. As a result there are often 75 to 100 ships waiting off-shore at a total cost to the HVCC of US$1.7 million per day. There is thus an urgent need to extend the progress made in relationship-building and management to the extremities of this supply chain. Only then will it be possible to realize the full value that this strategically important enterprise is capable of capturing and creating.

Typical symptoms of ineffective value creation

Typical symptoms of situations where this 'super' factor is not being performed effectively include:

- Recruitment and/or retention of partners is problematic.

- Intermediaries look to justify the need for higher margins to support product/service sales.

- Intermediaries cherry pick models.

- Overt conflict and frequent disagreements.

- Micro-management of operational metrics.

- Tactical programmes are used as a pricing tool.

- Partners' investment in the relationship is minimal.

- Senior management involvement is minimal.

- The partner seeks ongoing funding from the host to support any activity.

The model of partnership performance

As a total package, the three partnership 'super' performance factors (partnership quality, collaborative innovation and value creation) allow managers to make an objective evaluation of the overall relationship performance of a partnership or alliance. Chapter 5 demonstrated the technique of using surveys to gauge the views of managers on both sides of a partnership and to produce performance ratings based on their responses.

Table 6.4 shows how this can be used as a performance model for any partnership where each factor is jointly rated by the partners. This rating gives managers a set of simple metrics that can be monitored over time and used to drive performance improvement. This is especially the case when more detailed ratings are extracted from the factors' component parts and these are supported by diagnostics collected from interviews with selected, knowledgeable managers from each partner's team.

These are leading indicators that help us to predict the likelihood of a partnership being successful or not. They do not replace other conventional process output measures but they provide management with metrics and diagnostics to correct and improve key areas.

Table 6.4 The partnership performance model

Performance Factor	Performance Assessment			
Partnership quality				
Collaborative innovation				
Value creation				
Performance rating:	High	Medium	Medium-low	Low

Summary

This chapter has revealed that successful partnerships generate value as a consequence of the way in which the partners are innovative, manage the relationship within agreed standards of behaviour, and create and capture value through a focus on synergy and critical and positive self-evaluation. This has culminated in the development of a partnering performance model. The performance of relationships can be assessed in terms of the three 'super' factors that combine both relational and operational measures. In this way it is possible to gauge the 'total' performance of a partnership or alliance rather than the more customary and much more limited financial view. In the next chapter the practical application of this model in the Gibbs+Humphries Partnership Types is described.

Key action points

1. Consider collaborative innovation (adaption, innovation, communication and cooperation) in the context of your key commercial relationships. How do they score in your estimation: high, medium, medium-low or low?

2. Consider partnership quality (commitment and trust) in the context of your key commercial relationships. How do they score in your estimation: high, medium, medium-low or low?

3. Consider value creation (productive synergy, conflict management, value capture and efficiency) in the context of your key commercial relationships. How do they score in your estimation: high, medium, medium-low or low?

4. Review the symptoms identified for partnership quality, collaborative innovation and value creation. To what extent are they recognizable characteristics of your partnership(s)?

5. What are the commercial and management challenges for your firm as a consequence of these symptoms?

7 The Gibbs+Humphries Partnership Types

Introduction

In-depth assessments have been carried out of numerous partnership and alliance relationships with public sector and corporate organizations in the UK, Europe and internationally. These relationships have ranged from SMEs worth US$30 million per year to very large collaborative enterprises worth over US$3 billion per year. Analysis has been carried out using the scientific principles that underpin the ideas in this book and especially the partnership performance model described at the end of the last chapter. As a result, it is possible to identify and accurately characterize eight archetypal partnership types using high, medium, medium-low and low ratings for the three 'super' partnership success factors described in Chapter 6:

1. *Collaborative innovation* – the conditions that describe the effectiveness of the relationship and enable the partnership to be innovative and to respond to opportunities.

2. *Partnership quality* – the quality of the relationship including key behaviours like commitment and trust.

3. *Value creation* – the efficiency of the relationship to create and capture the potential value that the partnership offers.

Practically and pragmatically, therefore, business-to-business relationships predominantly fall into one of the following eight Gibbs+ Humphries Partnership Types:

1. Evangelists.

2. Stable Pragmatists.

3. Rebellious Teenagers.

4. Evolving Pessimists.

5. Captive Sharks.

6. Cherry Pickers.

7. No Can Dos.

8. Deserters.

This chapter describes each of the types so that you will be able to recognize those that you are involved in. Chapter 8 will detail how a practising manager can accurately assess the relationship type that best describes their business partnership(s) and offer some advice on how best to manage the situation in which you will find yourself.

Evangelists

Overview

Evangelists are firms that appear to be on an extended honeymoon for one or both of the parties involved in the partnership. The level of 'mindshare' and overall satisfaction is exceptionally high and 'word-of-mouth' references would be very positive. Quite often these are mature relationships that have become well established over time, but Evangelists can also be present among early adopters in a market or for a new product. They may also appear to be past their prime and 'living on old glories'.

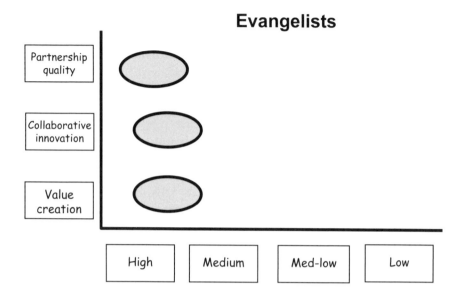

Figure 7.1 Evangelists

Recognizing Evangelists

Evangelists represent a conundrum within relationship types. Their self-assessment of the relationship will indicate that no factors could be improved and that there is complete collaborative harmony in the relationship. The level of trust is very high. An Evangelist will have the utmost belief in the host firm's abilities and competencies, as well as in their intention to operate in the best interests of the relationship. Commitment is similarly well established, especially in the area of common goals that exists between the partners. There is also likely to be a firm belief in the commercial benefits of the alliance to the extent that significant profit or revenue, or both, can be directly attributable to the partnership. The firms involved are likely to want to invest in structural elements of the partnership and as such Evangelists can be characterized by the level of training undertaken, the personnel resources allocated, and the IT linkages or the physical resources in place. Levels of coordination to organize and plan for cooperative activity will also be high, with much energy being devoted to driving collaborative initiatives.

However, it is here that the Evangelist myth starts to unravel. Research has shown that many Evangelists are not the largest or most profitable partners. Furthermore, while firms should aspire to building and improving the level of cooperation within a partnership, it is critically important that other aspects of a partnership are also worked hard. Importantly, this 'sharpness' cannot be completed without some constructive conflict. While Evangelists are very positive in terms of the partnership, they may become very inward-looking, and are often not market-connected to the extent that they will concentrate on the preservation of a partnership's promise when the commercial justification for it has ended. This might be explained away by the very strong social bonds that are typically present, but it can also be due to a situation where one party is heavily reliant on the other. Evangelists eventually do not perform very well in terms of creativity and innovation. There is a marked tendency for such partnerships to become sceptical and apprehensive about any factors that could upset the equilibrium of the partnership. Changes to the strategic structure of the relationship caused by an outside force, such as a parent company or head office, will usually produce a defensive reaction to bolster and maintain the status quo.

Although strengthening investments in a relationship is highly beneficial, if this is taken to excess over time it will make one or both partners effective hostages to the relationship. This can be a clear indication that an Evangelists' partnership is in decline. Process is also likely to play a major role in the management of this type of relationship. There may be agreements upon agreements of who does what, when and to whom that have built up over time. These have almost become an end in themselves. As a consequence there is likely to be some resistance to change and a degree of sluggishness in adapting to new conditions in the marketplace. Evangelist relationships are also identified by a lack of effective measures of performance. While reviews invariably take place they are unlikely to lead to the partners actively seeking ways for improvement or correction. It is therefore not uncommon for these partnerships to be burdened with outdated and complex management processes.

In summary, Evangelists may be very effective alliances but there is a danger of them becoming complacent. They are likely to be still 'riding their original success wave' but, at some point, they will begin to send out erroneous messages to the market (and themselves). This is when they have lost their edge and become inflexible and vulnerable to external changes. In their early days, Evangelists will produce super returns, ie 1+1=5 but this may 'burn-out' and result in a tail-off over time.

A tale of office supplies

The two firms involved in this supply chain relationship were long-established partners. The general manager of 'Office Supplies Co' had previously been the regional sales director for 'ManuCo'. The partnership operated in the mature office equipment sector in Germany where Office Supplies Co was a sales and marketing organization and ManuCo was a subsidiary of a specialized office equipment manufacturer. ManuCo was a moderately sized pan-European company with around 500 employees. Office Supplies Co was smaller and served a wide range of customer types but with a strong presence in the regional and local government sectors.

Office Supplies Co had a major showroom where ManuCo's products could be demonstrated and tested by potential customers. Approximately 20 per cent of Office Supplies Co's business was dependent upon ManuCo's products. Office Supplies Co represented less than 5 per cent of ManuCo's business in Germany but effectively had territory-exclusivity in the southern German states around Munich and Stuttgart.

The relationship was characterized by a lot of communication and exchange of information and close cooperation between the two firms, which would often work side by side in front of key accounts. The operational processes were often the cause of stories and jokes because it tended to be complex and very idiosyncratic. However, the staff in both firms had 'grown up' with it and it was not so much 'what you knew' but 'who you knew' in the other company that enabled things to get done.

Sales growth over the last four quarters had been particularly sluggish and the loss of a major customer had forced the firms to review the business model to try to work out what was going wrong. The review identified that Office Supplies Co was charging customers a premium price for the product that was above the market norm and, while existing customers were very satisfied with the quality of service, there was a growing concern that the overall package was becoming overpriced. The parties decided that the best way forward was an increase in all forms of marketing to showcase the benefits of their joint approach.

Coincidental to this situation a new European manager was appointed by ManuCo. The new manager began an expansion of the number of partners across Europe to increase market coverage. The immediate response was a closing of ranks within the German organization between Office Supplies Co and ManuCo. The European expansion initiative was seen as being unnecessary in Germany, and the local message of 'quality' of the solution not 'quantity' of sales points was re-emphasized. The initial coverage assessment was ignored, delayed, denigrated and finally undertaken under duress and, not surprisingly for the German management team, the results were inconclusive.

This cooperative marketing initiative was launched to the regional customer base at a top Munich hotel. A few journalists and customers came along but the overall reception was very lukewarm. Office Supplies Co decided that the best way forward was to increase the number of sales people and therefore, again supported by ManuCo, set about recruiting and training five new sales representatives. The results continued to be poor and, for the first time, the management teams started to be critical of their partner's operational competence. After six months, most of the newly recruited sales people (as well as some of the existing sales team) had left – some to competitors. The partnership between Office Supplies Co and ManuCo continued for a further 12 months until a series of contractual losses forced the appointment of a second and then a third regional partner. Within 18 months the partnership was terminated after an out-of-court settlement.

This transition from Evangelist to Deserter is not uncommon. Often the deserting Evangelist will display characteristics of a Captive Shark.

Stable Pragmatists

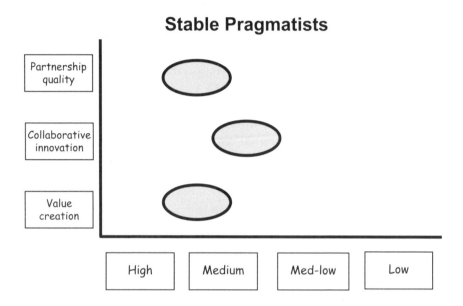

Figure 7.2 Stable Pragmatists

Overview

Stable Pragmatist relationships are usually found in fairly established markets and are characterized by cooperation based upon the pragmatic need to overcome the usual supply chain operating difficulties that 'go with the territory'. Culture-matching appears to have taken place, which has brought about a feeling of 'being in the same boat'. Relationship management and relationship building can be unstructured but effective, because managers are intuitively adept. Nevertheless, on the whole, the firms and the individuals involved understand the potential benefits of cooperation and the partnership functions at above average performance.

Recognizing Stable Pragmatists

These relationships can cover a span of situations. At the lower end there will be partnerships that have moved out of an adversarial zone into a situation of 'rubbing along' because the alternative is too painful. To use a marriage analogy, this is 'staying together for the sake of the children'. In the middle of the group there will be organizations that have achieved a reasonable level of efficiency but are unable or unwilling to put in the extra effort to do better. At the upper end of the Stable Pragmatists will be those alliances that have begun to overcome the internal and external difficulties they are facing and have the potential enthusiasm to become Evangelists. The common factor is that these relationships are pragmatically, realistically and proactively managed and consequently effective and productive.

Although both sides will be aware of the needs of their relationship and will periodically make efforts to improve performance, there will be the daily competition between short-term decisions on financial, operational and brand objectives, and taking joint partnership-oriented decisions. Another common phenomenon will be the lack of consistent relationship management direction across the partner organizations. There will be pockets of clarity, often at the top, with considerable variability in the rest of the companies. Enthusiastic individuals at lower levels may become frustrated because the organization doesn't seem to support apparently obvious actions which, if carried out, will bring clear partnership benefits. This can be disrupted by constant reorganizations and staff churn, which upset accountability and relationship-building efforts and generally get in the way of introducing new ideas. Innovation is thus a relatively weak point and it is often only possible to generate localized, short-term improvement initiatives in the relationship.

Nevertheless, and in the face of these difficulties, senior staff are particularly knowledgeable about the benefits of their partnering relationships and will accept that it is important to improve cooperation and to deal constructively with problems. This attitude will have filtered through the organizations but is often practised only with apologies when pressures of operational fire-fighting get in the way of joint behaviours. A mutual respect for the other side's problems and achievements and the way they sometimes have to do things that run counter to the partnership are often strong characteristics of Stable Pragmatists: 'They deliver even though they are inflexible and quirky.' Thus at the working level it is likely that the sides will work together on issues rather than formally complain, and commercial officers are likely to be relatively flexible when upholding the letter of the contract. These relationships generally get things done and many are long-lived – over 20 years, like 'old married couples'. They have usually reached a state of efficient equilibrium which, although are not as productive as it could be, produces above average returns.

Confectionery woes

The customer was a global confectionery manufacturer with multi-million dollar revenues. Approximately 20 years ago the European division decided that it would experimentally diversify into about 10 niche markets. To do this it identified capability within individual SMEs and began a partnering arrangement with each. Under the customer's guiding hand each SME developed its processes and capabilities and provided a valuable foothold in specialist markets.

From a family business that sold its products on local markets, the SME had, within the partnership, become a world-class manufacturer of seasonal confectionery. It had developed extremely innovative production techniques and through similarly clever supply chain management was able to reduce stockholdings and produce to order very flexibly. Moreover, without upsetting the arrangement with the customer, the supplier had become a major expert in its field and had lucrative contracts with most of the customer's competitors. Nevertheless, the relationship was so successful that the customer increased its dependence on the supplier to over 80 per cent.

Just after 2002 things began to change when the original customer 'entrepreneurs' moved on and the supplier's account was handed over to a small management team within the group that handled the main product lines. The SME found that its relationship was being managed by comparatively junior staff who, despite the simple, phased delivery contract, expected daily, detailed reports and did not have the authority to discuss product innovation and market development matters. The situation was compounded by the imposition of the customer's logistics organization, which was very capable of supplying to a major production line but had considerable difficulty meeting the supplier's highly flexible way of working. Problems grew as the logistics company's failures caused the supplier to miss production targets and, due to the lack of anyone willing to listen on the customer side, the supplier invoked penalty clauses in its contract. The supplier was, in effect, working to rule in order to draw attention to its difficulties.

Initially the customer carried out a market study to find a replacement supplier. However, it quickly realized that the current supplier's ability to deliver and innovate reliably and at some 40 per cent lower cost than other market players left it with no viable alternative. Senior customer staff then became involved and instigated a performance assessment of the relationship, which highlighted the compelling business case to retain the partnership and the underlying commitment by staff to support it. A review was then carried out of the supply chain processes that involved the customer, supplier and third-party logistics firm to improve understanding and seek solutions to the logistics problems. The customer invited the supplier to join it in regular product/market planning meetings with the intention of improving market share and lower costs to sell.

The customer realized that a very successful relationship had deteriorated through lack of care. Although the overall performance of the supplier had been maintained, process costs had increased and reduced staff morale had adversely affected innovation. It took five years for the customer to realize the scope of the problem and the need for joint efforts to begin the turnaround.

What the customer said:

'We respect them as an organization; they have their own challenges to face.'

'We have worked together for many years and the original feelings are still strong.'

'The relationship could deliver so much more so it's worth fighting to save.'

'They optimized part of their process but this added to our supply chain costs. They are very self-centred.'

'We are always coming under pressure because they don't plan until very late in the day.'

What the supplier said:

'We attended an away-day and bottomed out many problems. Sometimes we need to force these discussions to clear the air.'

'Product development has suffered because they wouldn't commit to a sole supply agreement. We are now working on a common platform that is helping.'

'The culture difference didn't used to matter. Now there is a clash.'

'It would work better if we each did what we are best at. Sometimes we are not chasing the same ball.'

'We are very passionate about what we do; this is why we sometimes get excited when supply chain problems affect us.'

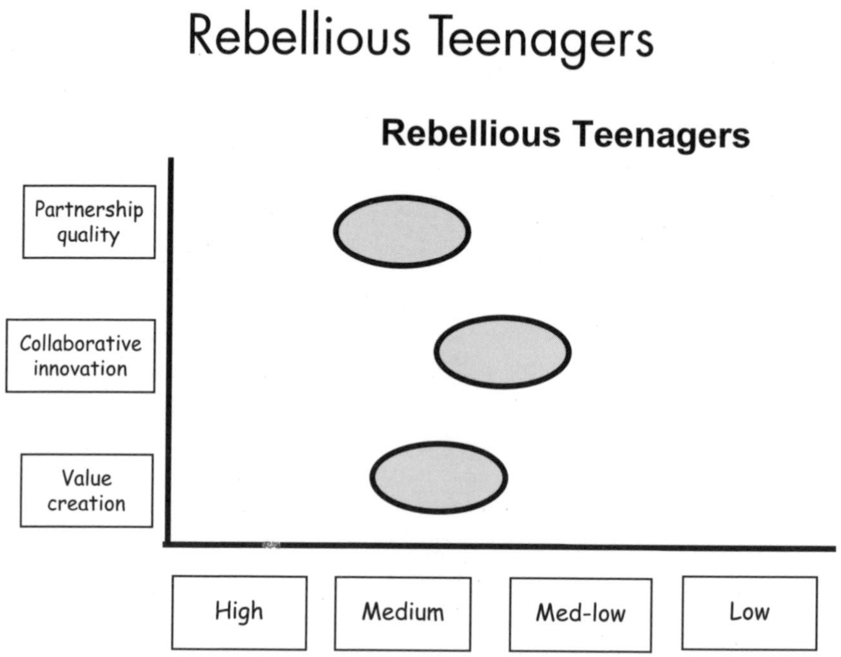

Rebellious Teenagers

Rebellious Teenagers

	High	Medium	Med-low	Low
Partnership quality	⬭			
Collaborative innovation		⬭		
Value creation	⬭			

Figure 7.3 Rebellious Teenagers

Overview

Rebellious Teenagers relationships are not uncommon, and often represent partnerships where the scale of contribution, performance and importance to both firms is high. They have typically been in existence for some time, although Rebellious Teenagers relationships can emerge from less mature partnerships. There is or at least has been a degree of mutual reliance in the relationships that over time is reducing and being replaced with attitudes (cultural or commercial) that are no longer wholly sympathetic to the original reasons for the alliance or partnership.

Recognizing Rebellious Teenagers

Rebellious Teenagers maintain a good working relationship with the host. This is supported by quite a high degree of trust. Rebellious

Teenagers trust the capabilities and competence of their partners as well as the people they do business with. This maintains the strength and durability of the relationship as well as commitment to it. Commitment is high because the firms are happy with the common goals and the prospect of achieving the sorts of commercial benefits that they desire. As a result they will continue to invest at a relatively high level and see these 'ties' and 'pledges' as essential acts that bind the partnership together. However, Rebellious Teenagers are restless partnerships and will become impatient for returns. If these are not satisfied in quantity and quality, then some acrimony can start to creep in. Rebellious Teenagers are always on the look out for imbalance in the contributions made by each partner and will become tetchy and petulant if they see that all is not precisely fair.

Despite the level of trust and commitment, there is thus conflict in these relationships. This arises because the Rebellious Teenager feels that the partner is not always being fair in its dealings (despite being reliable) and has objectives and ambitions that are not wholly compatible with the perceived common aims of the partnership. This situation can arise when a firm expands its strategic alliances or supply chain relationships and starts to engage with a competitor. The level of conflict is not disruptive to the partnership, but there is a tendency for queries and issues to fester. One cause of disagreement is the perception that the partner is not very flexible and that policies and processes are dictating too much of the relationship. Rebellious Teenager partnerships are often cited as being bedevilled by 'red tape' and there will be constant demands for more freedom of action such as decentralized decision making, greater local autonomy or more empowerment of boundary personnel. The partner is accused of being 'difficult to work with' and the Rebellious Teenager will argue for simpler processes. Constructive discussion is held back, however, because although heated debates take place, it is usually very difficult to agree on productive outcomes.

There is thus a problem with open dialogue and discussion, and Rebellious Teenagers will often blame their partners for not understanding their business model, or that their requirements have been misheard, misunderstood or ignored. The lack of two-way communication stands in contrast to the relatively high level of operational information-sharing that takes place. At this level there is openness in giving information about customers, market conditions or competitor activity. However, this does not help enable the parties to achieve a common understanding of how they can better work together and collaborate. Joint planning takes place, therefore, with a focus on numbers, targets and metrics, and results in documented plans that remain static and rarely fully put into practice. Cooperation is therefore not all-encompassing or efficient. Nevertheless, the Rebellious Teenager will express itself satisfied with the partnership because its main objectives are being achieved. However, in private it will complain that the level of profitability or ROI being captured is insufficient and that it is being held back by its partner.

The commercial consequence of such relationships is that the potential value that could be created is lost or not captured, ie 1 + 1 = 2.5 or 3. While the scale of business could be significant – it is not uncommon to find major partnerships displaying 'problem child' tendencies – the growth of the business is relatively low and stable. There are considerable inefficiencies in the management of these relationships as much effort is put into maintaining the social bonds and resolving short-term or tactical issues.

Ups and downs in IT

The two firms involved in this relationship had been working together for several years. One was a major IT manufacturer, the other was a large reseller that specialized in selling into the large corporate and governmental accounts. The manufacturer also operated its own direct sales force who sold into the same corporate accounts, but this sales organization focused on a different product set to the corporate reseller and up until recently there had been no conflict.

Both companies worked well together; there was a recognized synergy in sales management processes and the firms shared very similar organizational cultures: results focused and numbers driven. The companies also fully recognized the compatibility of their selling resources. The manufacturer could provide the system and the reseller provided the solution and service. This combination had resulted in several high profile sales contracts valued at millions of pounds. The partnership flourished in an environment of frequent information exchange and dialogue.

However, there was a thorn in the side of this harmony. The manufacturer's direct sales force had started to sell solutions and services to the large accounts. There was still a wall between the products that the direct sales organization sold and those available to the corporate reseller, but it did seem like the wall was getting paper-thin at times. This was particularly the case when the manufacturer suggested that they collaborate on a very high-end deal, which involved a wide range of products and services. The proposal was a simple one: the manufacturer would act in this instance as the prime supplier and sub-contract back to the corporate reseller for various elements of the service delivery. The margin available on the sub-contracted service would be high and therefore very profitable to the reseller. The corporate reseller remained trustful of the manufacturer's intentions but was sceptical of the benefits. The proposal went ahead but didn't meet with the client's approval and the deal was lost.

Over time several similar opportunities arose and the partners took turns to be the lead or sub-contractor. The success rate was acceptable, and though they lost more than they won, the profitability of the deals seemed to make it a viable strategy. Because of this, both firms remained outwardly committed to the partnership. Inwardly, however, the corporate reseller side was increasingly concerned about the cost of doing business this way and the longer-term commitment of the manufacturer to the partnership. The manufacturer was also less comfortable in its dealings with the corporate reseller, feeling that there was a risk that the corporate reseller might enter into similar arrangements with other suppliers.

The consequences were manifold. The business relationship continued to produce 1 + 1 = 3 results, although there was an undercurrent of conflict and less cooperative activity. More frequent formal reviews took place, with a less 'open book' approach to joint bid development. This often led to the proposals being under-cut in price and out of kilter with the market.

Evolving Pessimists

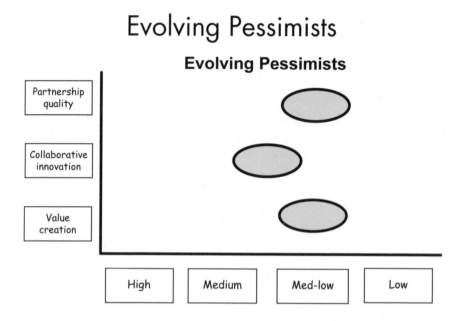

Figure 7.4 Evolving Pessimists

Overview

Evolving Pessimist relationships are clearly attempting to improve their performance. However, operating problems such as supply chain complexity, ill-fitting processes, inherent difficulties in predicting customer requirements and either cultural or financial obstacles to process and facility improvements are apparent, and these generally reduce the overall relationship satisfaction levels and returns. They may often be found in 'difficult' businesses such as defence and developing-world environments.

Recognizing Evolving Pessimists

Evolving Pessimist relationships exhibit many of the characteristics of No Can Dos. Difficult operating conditions resulting from unstable markets and having to support complex/unreliable products are likely to preoccupy managers. These problems will affect views of the risk, so relationship investments in infrastructure and people will be hard to justify. Moreover, short-termist behaviours, selfishness and opportunism will tend to undermine improvement initiatives. However, probably because of familiarity and prolonged experience with the operating problems, a certain perverse satisfaction is present and as a result morale has continued to hold up. Relationship conditions may therefore have reached an unhappy truce state or at least a reduction of active adversarial behaviours. Hence communication, especially surrounding joint problem solving, will take place and marginally raise the level of innovation, but although the will to cooperate is growing, the ability to translate this into reliable product and service delivery chains has yet to develop. Returns from these relationships will be below average, ie 1+1=2.

A ray of hope in avionics

The customer was a major UK airline with global operations. The supplier was a world leader in the design, manufacture and provision of maintenance services for avionic 'black-boxes'. The relationship, which involved the forecasting, repair, modification and replacement of aircraft avionic equipment, was over 14 years old and worth approximately £40 million per year. High penalty clauses came into effect if the lack of a module prevented an aircraft from meeting its schedule.

In the last six years the customer had been faced with very difficult market conditions including over-capacity and fierce competition from budget airlines. It had cut back on equipment support, expecting its supplier to make up the difference through greater efficiency. The latter was struggling to modernize its product range to meet increasingly strong competition from a civil market that was being 'invaded' by defence manufacturers. It in turn asked the customer to invest in new state-of-the-art cockpit instrumentation that was an order of magnitude more reliable and would secure its future in the forefront of a crucial aspect of the sector.

Communication between the partners became poor and both felt the other had lost touch with their strategic objectives. More importantly, although both 'took on board' the need for greater efficiency and the need to cut costs, these messages did not permeate consistently throughout the respective organizations. As a result, the teamwork that had characterized the early years of the relationship broke down and, for example, the supplier held spares progress meetings without a customer representative being present. Moreover, usage forecasting information from the customer became increasingly sporadic and was seldom up-to-date. Instead of holding regular performance review meetings, communication was increasingly conducted by e-mail and when meetings were held, twice a year, they were unproductive, acrimonious affairs with each side blaming the other for failures. The commercial staff became involved and twice penalty clauses were exacted on the supplier. The customer's adoption of a supplier relationship management strategy did not help the situation because it tended to 'talk down' to the supplier rather than treat it as a strategic partner.

Matters began to change when the supplier appointed a new key account manager. He realized that an impasse had been reached between the companies that was dragging each down and something was needed to break the cycle of negative behaviour. After all, neither side was able to contemplate the immense disruption that would be caused by severing the contract completely. He initially found it impossible to open a constructive dialogue with the customer; everyone was too busy solving other pressing problems. He therefore completely reorganized the customer support desk function within his company and offered price discounts where advance information was made available on item exchanges. He also encouraged his engineering and design personnel to instigate technical discussion meetings with the customer's maintenance staff. These became well attended because those intimately involved with the day-to-day struggle to provide serviceable equipment for aircraft had a close affinity.

Eventually, monthly spares progress and performance review and problem-solving meetings began to take place. The commercial officers were still present, but the threat of contract penalties had diminished. There was still considerable wrangling over investment in improving the information systems and other process linkages between the companies, but some small 'wins' had been achieved. Under pressure from the 'allied' technicians, a solid state altimeter was developed and purchased for all the aircraft of a particular type in the customer's fleets. This cut operating costs, and it was suggested that in the forthcoming review and renewal of the contract, some performance incentives would be introduced. There was a ray of hope within both companies that there could be a way out of a poor situation.

What the customer said:

'They never plan ahead, they are always reactive, and they promise much at the meetings but deliver very little in practice.'
'They often sit on work for two to three years and refuse to deliver the goods.'
'Their spares ordering point just seems to add more delay.'
'They don't seem to have the resources to chase their subcontractors who let them down.'
'We have given them numerous formal warnings but they seem to have no effect.'
'Their customer help desk actually provided me with useful information – I was shocked!'

What the supplier said:

'We seem to constantly fight fires; there seems to be no planning.'
'They don't seem to realize we have production schedules and cannot stop everything to satisfy their instant requirements.'
'They quibble over pennies and then take months to agree to the price.'

'There is a gulf in perception between the sides over performance.'

'Without a common understanding of how we are doing and what we must achieve we cannot move forward.'

'We engineers talk the same language; getting things fixed is what we do. We have no time for bickering over the contract.'

Captive Sharks

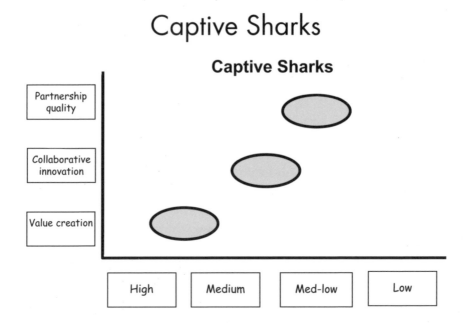

Figure 7.5 Captive Sharks

Overview

In a similar manner to Rebellious Teenagers, Captive Shark relationships often represent partnerships where the scale of contribution, performance and importance to both firms is high. It is the size of the business, the market position of the host firm or potentially contractual or market conditions that drives the relationship. The key descriptor of a Captive Shark is the very high level of commitment and dependency. This high commitment is matched by equally high levels of conflict and adversarial behaviour, which leads to low levels of collaboration.

Recognizing Captive Sharks

The relationship is marked by confrontational negotiation about obligations, service levels and, in supply chain and marketing channel relationships, margins and profitability. Surprisingly, trust is not necessarily very low overall. There is trust in the ability, competence and reputation of the partner, but Captive Sharks will be distrustful of the partner's longer-term objectives and ambitions, seeking a hidden agenda in most if not all situations and concerned whether the host firm has its best interests at heart.

The Captive Shark will normally have invested substantially in the partnership, and will cite a lack of investment by the other partner as a sign of a lack of fairness. This difference may or may not be a true reflection of reality, but nevertheless influences its behaviour. There is also an undercurrent that the partnership does not share a true set of common objectives, apart from at a very basic level, ie gain large revenue or market share. This lack of common ground leads to frequent conflicts that can be intense and drawn out and permeate throughout the whole organization, from senior management downwards. This leads to anecdotes and stories about the duplicity or deviousness of one or other partners, which can become part of the culture within the firms and the partnership. Almost in contradiction there is a high level of social bonding and communication in many of these partnerships; but the extent of actual open discussion and the sharing of information is very low. In these partnerships information is seen as a weapon to use in negotiations, and the Captive Shark is reluctant to give away anything without immediate gain or scoring a point.

These are not comfortable relationships and therefore it is not surprising that collaboration is not effective; return on investment can be low and margins slim, ie $1 + 1 = 2.5$. There can often be a very high focus on processes, performance metrics and discussions about roles and accountabilities that impede joint planning and getting things done. The relationships are marked by a lack of real or perceived reliability as hard-won concessions are often subsequently retracted or countered, or commitments to action delayed or overtaken by other events. The firms involved will often be relatively inflexible, preferring to keep within relatively tight operational boundaries and resorting to contracts or service levels as the benchmark against which success is measured. The Captive Shark will feel that the other partner is simply not doing enough to support the sales or marketing activities of the partnership. Actual levels of operational communication will typically be high, reflecting the scale or significance of the partnership, but the levels of expectations are also high and a 'lack of real communication' is often cited as a critical deficiency.

The key to understanding these relationships lies in the strength of the product, service, brand, or market position that one or both parties represent. The very substantial economic proposition that initiated the partnership in the first place continues to sustain it despite all the negative behaviours described above. Captive Sharks are not overly dissatisfied with the relationship; in fact in many ways they are satisfied and accept the disagreements as a 'fact of life'. Many large-scale alliances share the characteristics of Captive Sharks, and such alliances can be major forces in the marketplace to the extent that competing against them can be a very painful experience.

Eight hundred pound gorillas

This strategic alliance involves two major international organizations. They are supply chain partners, and both can be described as '800 pound gorillas'. In their respective sectors they are the dominant players; they have the products/services and brand strength to command respect. Their alliance was founded on the basis of a mutual need to exploit the significant commercial capabilities that each offered.

The relationship was characterized by adversarial negotiations on everything from targets and rebates to service levels and whatever the subject. These disagreements would spiral up and down throughout the organization and often 'leak' into the trade press as a story about the imminent dissolution of the partnership. In reality the level of commitment by both firms was exceedingly high. Both firms recognized that the scale of the commercial enterprise would not be easy to replace. To manage the business between them the firms had invested in processes and IT solutions that were wholly dedicated to the purpose. Both firms also had teams of people assigned to managing the partnership who would occupy desks in their partner's offices or warehouses. These resources were present throughout the organizations, both within field operations as well as within the main international and European headquarters.

As a consequence, the level of social bonding was high. People knew one another, and yet despite this familiarity the level of open dialogue and collaboration was low. Both firms were on the constant look out for opportunities to take advantage of any signs of weakness in the other.

The firms had very structured review procedures that were based exclusively on a set of performance metrics. These perform-ance metrics were detailed, complex and exhaustive. In fact disagreements regularly occurred on the relevance, calculation and causes of these metrics. Monthly reviews would feed into quarterly reviews, quarterly reviews would feed into the annual plan, and daily operational reporting would be scrutinized to build the monthly 'management slide decks'.

This partnership was very successful on one side (operational performance) and yet was not profitable for either of them. This lack of profitability was a major source of disagreement, not because of the value lost, but because both parties thought that the other was or at least should be making significant returns on the business and was 'letting the side down'. It was this belief that the other party was actually making a profit, when one firm was making a loss, that was the spur to much friction.

In reality, despite the length and closeness of the relationship, neither party had taken the time to test fundamental assumptions about the business model of the partnership. Each multinational firm had its own process for generating and measuring profit and inferred this model onto its partner. As a consequence, while the short-term likelihood of partnership dissolution was low, both firms were eagerly and constantly exploring opportunities to replace the other partner.

Cherry Pickers

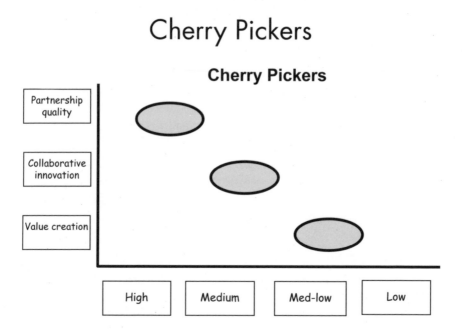

Figure 7.6 Cherry Pickers

Overview

Cherry Pickers are epitomized by their lack of commitment to the relationship, dependency upon the host firm or the beneficial outcomes of the partnership. Typically they will be seen as a good and reliable partner with whom there are few major concerns or areas of conflict. Their level of overall satisfaction is also relatively high and this can confuse management into believing that growth can be anticipated. In fact these partnerships will rarely produce stellar performance; collaboration will be half-hearted and investment in the relationship low. Levels of returns will only be average, ie 1 + 1 = less than 3.

Recognizing Cherry Pickers

The level of commitment within Cherry Pickers is generally low. They are particularly sceptical about the strategic significance of their partnership to longer-term growth and development. The view of the contribution of the partnership to the Cherry Picker's operational or financial performance will be moderate. Both firms will not consider major investments in their relationship but neither will be put out by this. The firms will trust each other's reputation and abilities, but social contact will be limited to the conference room.

The Cherry Picker will not see any commonality of goals within their partnerships. Interviews with such firms have received an almost blank look when asked whether common goals exist; the Cherry Picker simply does not see the relevance or need for such elements in a commercial transaction. At the same time, the level of conflict will be low, and an assessment is made simply on the ability of the partner to resolve queries and issues quickly and efficiently. This is not to suggest that partnership behaviour is not taking place. In Cherry Picker relationships the ability of the partner to perform in line with the expectations of the other is taken for granted and greater emphasis is placed upon the efficiency of the processes involved.

The level of collaboration is as a result very low and the ability of the partnership to generate operational benefits anything above the average is very restricted. Information sharing is pared back to the absolute minimum and two-way dialogue that would normally build the foundation for joint planning is non-existent. As such, joint planning is wholly focused on targets and service level metrics. Typical symptoms seen in many such relationships are inertia and a lack of innovation in driving the business forward. With little or no ambition to develop the partnership, the focus is on the immediate opportunity and how to capture it with little or no risk.

The Cherry Picker is not overly satisfied with the economic proposition represented by the firm or the partnerships. The product or service is ok, the brand or market position is ok, and the profitability or operational efficiency is ok. Nothing impresses the Cherry Picker, which will work with the partner when the situation or end-customer dictates.

Cherry Picker partnerships appear always to have the potential to develop further. The opportunity they represent can be substantial and yet never fully realized or brought to fruition. Such relationships occur in roughly one or two out of 10 partnerships, rarely more. Frequently the revenue represented by them is not large and yet the opportunity can be significant such that they could be considered a prize worth chasing.

Uncertain allies

There are approximately 65,000 resellers in the European IT market, selling everything from solutions and systems to laptops and printers. For a major IT manufacturer this channel represented its sole route to market. In 2004 it sold its products (via distributors) to nearly 10,000 of these resellers. Its market share was stable and its products recognized as being premium priced and high quality. During 2005, the IT market in this sector was subject to significant price erosion and a tightening credit squeeze. Nevertheless, unit sales of the products continued to grow, but in the face of a 15 per cent price fall, the firm was only able to hold flat its revenue and saw a decrease in its average margin and profitability.

During the same period the number of active resellers fell significantly, and a simple trend analysis showed that this decline had in fact been underway for the previous two years. The firm's analysis revealed that the average frequency of purchase by these resellers was also falling. Instead of an average of 10 units per month, these intermediaries were now selling less than eight units per month. On the understanding that averages always mask reality, the firm dug deeper. Three key factors emerged: 45 per cent of resellers were continuing to resell the products but their sale value had fallen sharply, and they were only purchasing on an infrequent basis. The firm had lost several thousand resellers which, having purchased in 2004, had not acquired any products in 2005.

A series of focus groups was conducted to determine the causes of this trend. The responses were equally revealing:

'The products are ok. They're pretty good in fact but the range is incomplete.'
'The products are premium priced, which makes them difficult to sell, and therefore the actual profitability is low.'
'I don't know anyone at the firm; I only speak to the distributor.'
'I have a couple of customers who really like these products, but none of my other customers is interested.'
'Yes, we did sell the products, but only one or two I think... I don't think we sold more, did we?'
'I would have been interested in working with the firm but I couldn't see where they were heading.'
'I typically put this firm's products on my proposals, simply to give an alternative – once in a while someone bites – unless I can avoid it.'

The firm's channel was awash with Cherry Pickers, many of whom had already deserted as times had grown tougher. The ones that remained were unfamiliar and unconvinced by the firm's value proposition and had not made any investment in time or energy to find out more. On the other side, the firm had been idle in pursuing this latent opportunity, preferring to concentrate on its more loyal and stable channel partners.

No Can Dos

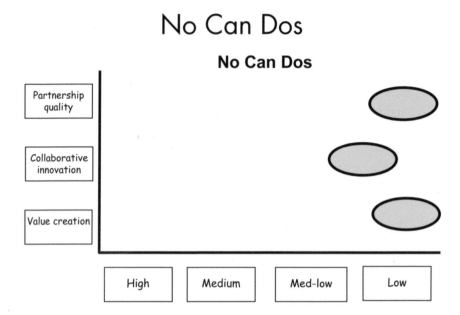

Figure 7.7 No Can Dos

Overview

Within No Can Dos, adversarial conditions are standard and since the opportunities to escape are very slim, they create strong feelings of 'imprisonment' and 'impotence'. A long-term lack of cooperation and entrenched opposition to any form of innovation also saps relationship vitality. Efforts to improve or gain better shares of the benefits are wasted. The result is poor supply chain practices and processes, and poor returns.

Recognizing No Can Dos

In No Can Do relationships adversarial behaviour is usually a reaction to feelings of being 'hemmed-in' in a relationship that limits the partners' management options and their ability to control their destiny. These feelings of 'imprisonment' and 'impotence' promote short-term risk-avoidance behaviours that lower commitment to investment in essentials such as infrastructure, IT, training and people. The knock-on effect is to do the least necessary to satisfy the contract. As a result, innovation is suppressed and cooperation on product or service quality, cost control and lowering joint risks will suffer. There are the inevitable consequences for customer satisfaction. Managers will find themselves 'fire-fighting' operational difficulties and joint problem solving will end up as squabbles over the contract small print with threatened recourse to penalty clauses. Self-interest and opportunism will quench trust like hot metal plunged into cold water. There will be an absence of sharing important information such as planning forecasts and IPR, and there may even be instances of deliberate obfuscation – being 'economical with the truth' – to gain advantage. The overall result is further insecurity, instability, cynicism and the pressures from confinement in an 'unhappy marriage'. There may be efforts to break out of this cycle but the lack of cooperation or alternatives will make this extremely difficult to achieve. The overwhelming attitude of the partners in this impossibly 'take it or leave it' situation is 'no can do', and returns are likely to be less than 1+1=2.

Old problems in UK defence

The No Can Do attitude is redolent of UK defence equipment contract relationships of the 1960s, 1970s and 1980s. It was widely believed that industry was making inordinately high profits by taking advantage of its technically naïve customer. Many projects had been years late, had delivered unreliable weapons systems and were vastly over-budget – for example the Nimrod Airborne Early Warning aircraft cancelled by Margaret Thatcher in 1986. Despite the customer's penchant for optimistic over-ordering (numbers that usually had to be cut back later due to budget constraints), underestimating technical difficulty and changing requirements at will, political distrust of industry's motives led to the introduction of a Cost-Plus policy. This was to be implemented by 'heavyweight' people like Sir Peter (now

Lord) Levene. This meant that the Ministry of Defence (MoD) would only pay industry's costs plus a set profit level. Feeling that they were inadequately compensated for the very high risks involved in developing leading-edge technology products, some companies made efforts to inflate their customer's view of their costs through various stratagems such as the declaration of unverifiable 'extras' in their accounts. In response, MoD inspectors were positioned on every production line to ensure that quality and production levels were maintained and the scope for 'cheating' was minimized. Companies felt that this practice was an unwarranted intrusion that increased bureaucracy and showed a lack of trust. It was then alleged that they made design short-cuts because these would not be spotted by the inspectors and would gain them long-term revenues from supplying spares and repairs for the unreliable systems.

The adoption of restrictive practices on both sides reduced the open exchange of ideas on joint innovation, which promoted risk aversion and short-term policies in an environment where the development of weapon systems took years and required entirely the opposite attitude. Moreover, the 'them and us' culture generated an approach to contracting that focused on the small print in an attempt to cover all contingencies and was characterized by adversarial commercial staff whose dysfunctional aims permeated the rest of the relationship. In consequence, company shareholders gained poor returns and the military customers ended up with rifles that stopped firing in the heat of battle.

Although considerable joint efforts have achieved significant improvements in the last 10 years of 'smart acquisition', the No Can Do culture still persists today in some parts of MoD/industry relationships.

What the customer said:

'We are under great pressure to reduce our costs but the firm takes advantage of its sole supplier position by over-charging for proprietary items.'

'"Take it or leave it" is their attitude.'

'We both realize that the only way forward is to partner, but the firm has had its own way for so long that it is very reluctant to change.'

'Its ethos is rooted in the past.'

'They drag their feet over product improvements because they know greater reliability will reduce their earnings on repairs.'

'We have regular order progress meetings, but they never fulfil their promises or reply to our requests for information.'

'We feel we are making all the moves to improve the relationship but they are not reciprocated.'

What the supplier said:

'They don't know what they want so how can we react properly to their requirements?'

'They don't have a focus in their organization to deal with us either. We offered them a terminal from our system so they could check progress, but their security people turned it down.'

'They provide no information so we can plan ahead.'

'The uncertainty makes it hard to concentrate on customer service.'

'I haven't even met the end-customer.'

'At the lower levels their staff aren't well trained.'

'It's galling to know my people know more about their jobs than they do.'

'When we first got our teams together we put all the issues on the wall and agreed to change the relationship; they now seem to have forgotten all their good intentions.'

Deserters

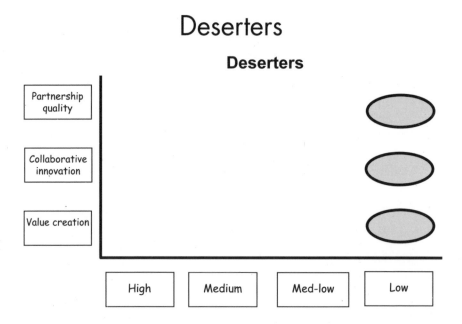

Figure 7.8 Deserters

Overview

While Evangelists see no 'bad' in the partnership, Deserters see no 'good'. Across all measures their assessment of the relationship is poor. No element of partnership meets with their approval and the extent to which business aims are achieved is minimal; collaboration per se is almost non-existent. Nevertheless it should not be assumed that these firms or organizations are operating at a purely trans-actional level. The quality of the relationship, their experience and expectations of their partner's behaviour to them, is important. The level of dependency and commitment is low and, as their name suggests, these firms are typically most likely to desert.

Recognizing Deserters

For many Deserters their current assessment of the relationship is a disappointment because at some point in the recent past it was either better or they had expectations that have not been realized.

These are therefore rarely new partnerships, but have probably been in existence for some time. Examples of their poor experience with the partner are cited in anecdotal evidence that highlights the lack of trustworthiness and reliability of the other firm. These complaints can often be directed at an individual or account manager, and this is partially reflected overall in a lack of interpersonal trust. The level of investment in the relationship by the partner is considered low, while the level of investment by the recipient firm is also low. As can be expected, the extent to which open two-way communication takes place is also very low.

The Deserter no longer believes that common goals exist between the partners or that the partner takes any of its interests into account when determining strategy or policy changes. The level and intensity of conflict is above the average but not exceptionally high. The frequency of disagreements is, however, very high, with incidents fuelling the discontent on a weekly and almost daily basis.

Collaboration overall is very poor. There is a perception that little or no coordination, planning or cooperation takes place and as a result there is a lack of sales and marketing activity. Similarly, Deserters believe they are constantly kept in the dark and cite the inaccuracy or lateness of notifications of key process or product/ service changes as examples. However, their opinion is often coloured by their views of the relationship as a whole and thus any suggestion of improvements in operations are mostly doomed to failure. The Deserter is increasingly disappointed by the fundamental economic aspects of the relationship. The reputation and brand of the partner is seen as riddled with flaws, the product or service is short in functionality or competitive advantage, and the overall profitability of the proposition is low.

It is probably a lack of economic performance in the first place that starts the downward spiralling of the Deserter. High expectations in terms of sales, margin or gains in market share that fail to materialize lead the Deserter to distrust other aspects of the partner's offering. The Deserter starts to consider the extent to which it wants or can commit to the partnership; concerns are raised about profitability and costs. Perceived untrustworthiness or lack of responsiveness from the partner (often funnelled through the account manager or alliance manager) reinforce negative opinions about the firm. Eventually there is a high probability that the relationship will be terminated.

The ending of this type of relationship is usually based on litigation or an explosive dénouement of the partnership. Typically, Deserters slip into the background, making fewer and fewer calls to the other firm and distancing themselves from meetings, conferences or other social activities. Not all Deserters actually desert. Some can be turned around while others remain long-term discontents. These residual Deserters bemoan the inadequacies of the relationship, yet continue to work as partners at arm's length and at low levels of operational performance.

Ships that pass in the night

Curiously, most firms fail to recognize their own Deserters when their level of dissatisfaction is in reality very apparent.

Interviewer: 'Can I start by asking, from your point of view, whether you see the relationship with [firm] as successful or not?'

Deserter: 'Not at present, we're finding it very tough. They've changed our rebates and targets so much that it's hard to see how we are going to make a profit this year. The products are simply not delivering and we have a lot of issues with them at present which maybe I shouldn't go into.'

Interviewer: 'What things make a difference to you in terms of the relationship?'

Deserter: 'Over the years we have invested heavily in working with [firm]. At times you get the feeling that [firm] thinks that they own you. They can be very arrogant in the way that they put pressure on you to sign up for things. At the end of the quarter or at the end of the year the pressure on us to help [firm] make their numbers is very intense. Quite simply they try and bully us to take stock in, even when we don't want to. But at the end of the day we can normally get them to give us extra rebates or more time to pay. It's crazy. It's silly business management. Everyone realizes it and yet we all do it. You get the feeling that they come here to try and stuff us and then think they've done a great job. It's stupid; all we do is take the stock at extra discount and then dump it out onto the market the next month or so. They simply don't have an understanding of how a small business works and they think they are so clever at managing us. Look, I'm committed to this business, to my business, not to [firm]. They get the two confused at times and think that I will do things for the greater good of [firm]. What do they think I am?'

The firm's account manager: '"John" is a good guy. We've been working together for years. He often has a bit of a moan and I normally have to push him hard for the numbers, but he always delivers. He often asks to see my boss. So once in a while, we take "John" out for a round of golf and patch up our differences'.

Needless to say the reseller terminated the long-term contractual relationship with the firm in question within six months of the interview. In this situation there was an overt reliance on the combination of contractual and (a misplaced belief in) strong social contacts to sustain the relationship and make it a success. Underlying the problem was a complete lack of appreciation of the business aims or issues of the partner.

Summary

This chapter has presented eight archetypal partnership or alliance types. Each is quite clearly different and case studies have been used to provide example situations to bring them to life. There are doubtless other types, but these are unlikely to be generic or widely applicable. Their value is two-fold. First, they represent recognizable situations that allow managers to understand what is happening and why. Secondly, they provide an opportunity to plan ahead; if you don't know your exact position, how can you map a route to your objective? However, these values will not be fully realized unless they are addressed jointly with your business partners. The next chapter will show how a manager may assess his or her organization's key relationships and categorize them according to the Gibbs+Humphries Partnership Types. Chapter 8 also provides guidance and direction for the management of each of the relationship types.

Key action points

1. At the end of Chapter 6 we asked you to plot the performance of your important partnerships and alliances using quality, innovation and value as your benchmarks. Now, compare those charts with the Gibbs+Humphries Partnership Types – Evangelists, Stable Pragmatists, Rebellious Teenagers, Evolving Pessimists, Captive Sharks, Cherry Pickers, No Can Dos and Deserters.

2. Note down the key points in your relationships that match our archetypal types.

3. Set out the high-level actions that will encourage improved partnering behaviours.

8 Making partnerships and alliances work for you

Management implications

Three critical messages have been identified for operational management, each of which is on one level intuitive, but in practice it is possible to quantify and substantiate them. The first point is that a firm's partnerships can form a key element of its overall strategic strength and make a very positive contribution to its financial and operational performance. The second point is that the quality of the relationship that firms have with their supply chain partners, their marketing channel and their strategic alliances, is critical to the success of their commercial endeavour. Third, a firm's business-to-business relationships can be categorized into eight major types. Each of these types displays a relatively unique set of characteristics and accompanying symptoms that can be managed in an appropriate way.

Having an understanding of relationship types is a major tool to help firms improve the effectiveness of their commercial partnerships. This chapter looks at how firms can undertake their own self-assessment of strategically important relationships so they can be characterized according to the Gibbs+Humphries Partnership Types. As already mentioned, unless managers can understand the key elements of partnership performance characteristics, they have little chance of managing it correctly. This chapter then looks at which account management practices and marketing initiatives could be best deployed to manage these different types of partnerships through the different phases of a product or market lifecycle.

At the end of each chapter a series of key action points has been set out. These are designed to challenge the reader to think 'outside of the box' and to test his or her paradigms or ideas. Reviewing these points in their entirety will allow the 'thinking manager' to make an initial assessment of the status and maturity of partnering strategies and operations. This initial self-assessment lays the foundation for the exercise described below.

Determining the right partnership type

The challenge confronting managers working with partners is being able to recognize in which category each of your partnerships fits so that effective management plans can be put in place. A detailed series of metrics and surveying techniques can be used to provide a diagnostic understanding of a partnership or alliance. However, the purpose of this final chapter is to provide a simple set of tools that help thinking managers to do this quickly and effectively for themselves.

Each of the relationship types is defined in terms of an extensive set of metrics. To make it easier to carry out a self-assessment, each partnership can be considered in terms of three factors:

1. The reference-ability of the partnership.

2. The effectiveness of the partnership.

3. The value to the businesses.

Self-assessment step 1

The first step is to consider your partnership in terms of how much you believe the following statements are applicable and to rate them in terms of high, medium, medium-low and low:

1. Reference-ability – our partner would provide us with a positive and flattering reference to a key customer or buyer.

2. Partnership effectiveness – in the last six months we have increased the level of satisfaction of our customers as a direct consequence of this partnership.

3. Value to the business – we have seen a real cost advantage/margin gain as a result of working with this partner *or* we represent a significant share of this partner's business.

This will help you to very roughly position a particular relationship within a G+H Type using Table 8.1.

Table 8.1 Self-assessment matrix 1

G+H Types	Reference-ability	Partnering effectiveness	Value significance
Evangelists	High	High	High
Rebellious Teenagers	High	Medium-low	Medium
Stable Pragmatists	Medium	Medium-low	Medium
Captive Sharks	Low	Medium	High
Cherry Pickers	High	Medium	Low
Evolving Pessimists	Medium-low	Medium-low	Medium-low
No Can Dos	Low	Medium-low	Low
Deserters	Low	Low	Low

Self-assessment step 2

The second step is slightly more difficult. For this step you need to think about what symptoms or behaviour support the assessment you made in step 1 in terms of each factor. These symptoms or behaviour are likely to relate to some of the following:

1. Reference-ability – commitment to the partnership over the longer term; common goals and aspirations; trust in the fairness of the partnership.

2. Partnership effectiveness – the ability of the partnership to innovate and adapt to new opportunities; communication effectiveness and openness; the willingness and ability to cooperate.

3. Value to the business – the speed and efficiency at solving problems and issues; capturing new customers, better profits, etc; improving processes.

Table 8.2 has been completed with example symptoms/behaviours.

The more positive symptoms that are observable the more likely it is that the relationship is performing at a higher level of satisfaction to the partner.

Self-assessment step 3

In the third step you need to consider whether there is any factual evidence that explains (causes) the symptom or behaviour that you have observed. See the example in Table 8.3.

Steps 2 and 3 are qualitative steps that should help you to draw out specific themes that characterize your relationship with your partner. These steps are also iterative with step 1; that is, you are likely to go back and make some adjustments to your original evaluation in the light of the symptoms and causes that you identify. The more symptoms and causes that you can identify in any area the greater will be the accuracy of your initial assessment in step 1.

These three steps will give you a rough idea of the sort of characteristics that describe your relationship and so help you position it in one or other of the eight relationship types. Once armed with this orientation it is recommended that you review the fuller description

Table 8.2 Self-assessment matrix 2

Symptom	Reference-ability	Partnering effectiveness	Value significance
1.	We have done joint PR with them	Repeat business is growing	Sales have doubled
2.	They invited us to present at their conference	Market share has grown	Margins have reduced slightly
3.	The number of joint customer visits is increasing	We have entered new markets together	We have extended our/their offering or range
4.	They have reduced their association with our competitor	We have joint process re-engineering initiatives underway	
5.		They always complain about our poor communication	
6.			
7.			
Total positive and negative symptoms	4 positive symptoms	4 positive symptoms 1 negative symptom	2 positive symptoms 1 negative symptom

Table 8.3 Self-assessment matrix 3

Reference-ability	Cause 1	Cause 2	Cause 3
Symptom 1 We have done joint PR with them	We have launched a new product/ service offering that we developed together		
Symptom 2 They invited us to present at their conference	We supported their annual sales conference and presented them with the 'Best in class' award		
Symptom 3 The number of joint customer visits is increasing	We have invested in some joint advertising which is producing more sales leads	We have better close sales force collaboration	
Symptom 4 They have reduced their association with our competitor	Our share of wallet has increased significantly	There was a contractual disagreement with the competitor	

of the specific relationship type and think about what actions are appropriate in the context of your business. Management options will be discussed in more detail later.

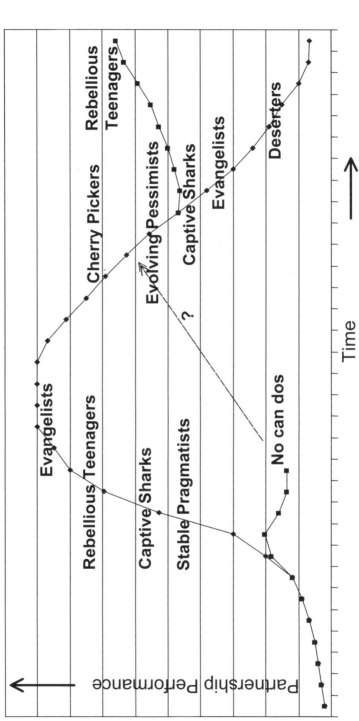

Figure 8.1 Market development chart

Partnership types and market development

Commercial activities tend to follow a normal course of events: from the early days of market entry, through the growth phase, maturity and then decline. In each of these phases all types of relationships are present, as shown in Figure 8.1. Deserters can be present at the very early phase of an alliance programme and Stable Pragmatists can be present in the period of decline.

However, it is possible to associate typical behaviours of partners with the phases of product or market development. It is more likely that early phases of development will be assisted by the presence of Evangelists who are prepared and willing to make sacrifices in terms of resources and time in the new opportunity in their inherent belief in its value. As we have already suggested, the growth phase can be accompanied by an increase in the number of Rebellious Teenagers. These relationships are very tense and yet the strength of the relationship enables them to work through conflict (changes in policy or strategy) and deliver innovative solutions.

Evangelists can be considered as the 'early adopters' in the life-cycle. As a firm starts to experience rapid growth, partnerships will see tensions arising as processes and strategies change to adapt to the different conditions. Rebellious Teenagers are likely to be present and can be a driving force in developing the business. Stable Pragmatists are also present and these are the partnerships that are likely to drive the business across the 'chasm' and into the mature phase of the lifecycle. These may be joined by reformed No Can Dos.

Typically, Captive Sharks would be expected to emerge during the mature stage of the partnership when the level of investment and commitment is at its highest, communication is fragmented and the need to sustain the growth or avoid decline puts pressure on the partnership.

As the market starts to enter its decline, Cherry Pickers will start to trade off the established brand and product strengths of the firm without making overt commitments to the partnership. Difficulties experienced during decline will bring about lowering levels of commitment and trust, which are associated with Evolving Pessimists.

Captive Sharks are seen as prevalent during the late phase as they struggle to find ways to extricate themselves from the relationship.

As the product or market enters decline, Deserters will come to the fore as partners become wholly dissatisfied with the commercial and operational realities. As a market or product gets beyond the 'sell by date', Evangelists will typically be the dominant type and sometimes the only relationships still present. While these will hold the partnership together, they are unlikely to support or enable any significant resurgence. Perhaps counter-intuitively, a decline can be stabilized and even turned back to a slight growth through a partnership with a Rebellious Teenager. In this instance the high level of functional conflict can enable a new market niche to be developed profitably through the combined efforts of the firms involved.

Relationship management and the Gibbs+Humphries Partnership Types

An understanding of the nature and characteristics of a partnership, or in the case of marketing channels, a series of partnerships, can help the relationship and channel managers decide the most appropriate action plan to manage in order to increase both effectiveness and productivity.

Managing Evangelists

The case study in the previous chapter identified some critical symptoms of Evangelists. These relationships can often be incestuous, with managers transitioning between the two organizations. It is not uncommon to find Evangelists charging premium prices and offering top-rank services.

Partnerships with Evangelists do not last for ever and often end acrimoniously. Introducing new initiatives into evangelistic partnerships is unlikely to succeed unless a detailed and factual assessment of the commercial realities has been carried out. Such an evaluation can lead to the realization that there is a lack of commercial gain in the performance of the partnership, which necessitates change. In strategic alliances, formalized approaches like lean six sigma can be used to ensure that the parties feel change is not being foisted upon them. Alternatively, a firm might decide that a reduction in the level of investment is appropriate.

While a change in management is sometimes an option for dealing with Evangelist partners, this can be a bumpy ride for the manager in question. A different approach could be to shift the leadership style away from participative to a more directional stance: setting targets, in-process metrics, tougher SLAs, etc. Managers within evangelistic relationships can sometimes become 'blind' to what is actually going on or going wrong. It is not uncommon to see investment being pumped into Evangelists despite the fact that the return might not be justifiable. Evangelists in the main are satisfied with the level of investment on both sides.

Evangelists thrive in stable environments where the need for change or disruption is low. They are also present in new markets and in new ventures where they are willing and prepared to commit resources into uncertain if not risky enterprises. Evangelists sometimes take the form of early adopters and can provide the foundation for market development; however, Evangelists should not be expected to help firms to 'jump the chasm' as their need and support for the status quo does not represent a growth mechanism.

Finally, in some instances, recognizing the existence of an evangelistic relationship can be a benefit in itself. The firm can leverage this overt support to test and trial new approaches jointly with the partner in the knowledge that the inherent strength will typically sustain the underlying relationship.

Managing Stable Pragmatists

A common feature of Stable Pragmatists is the strong desire to make their relationships work even though in practice the right effort is not always applied. They are not generally failing, just not performing as well as they could, and it is highly likely that the current position results from a lack of management attention and keeping up with change.

The secret to improving the quality of Stable Pragmatists is a more systematic approach to relationship management. Larger companies may have invested in a dedicated alliance function, while smaller firms have given a senior manager the additional responsibility of overseeing the conduct of the partnership portfolio. This role or function should not be the secondary task of the commercial or sales departments, nor should it be diffused across any departments that have a 'finger in the partnership pie'. It needs to have a central perspective where it can inform and be informed by strategic direction at board level.

Managing Rebellious Teenagers

It is important to recognize that Rebellious Teenagers maintain a 'buy-in' to the aims and objectives of the partnership. They can represent important allies that will remain loyal over time and will willingly come to the aid or support of the host or partner firm. It is therefore worthwhile to continue to nurture and develop them. In some instances Rebellious Teenagers represent the best candidates for moving into the growth and development phase of an opportunity (as compared to the initial or mature phase of a market). As a consequence of their challenging nature, Rebellious Teenagers can be sufficiently innovative and creative to realize new market opportunities.

What really drives the aims and aspirations of Rebellious Teenagers? They are usually trusting, social 'animals' so this should be relatively easy to tap into. However, quite often Rebellious Teenagers will only say what they think you want to hear in support of the partnership rather than their actual concerns and issues. Unless recognized, this concealment can be a real impediment to partnership success. The objectives of the partnership should be restated and framed in the context of the strengths and weaknesses of both parties. Joint initiatives can be instigated to improve operational efficiencies such that the Rebellious Teenager is providing the 'voice of the customer' input to process change or lean six sigma programmes.

A reappraisal and audit of the relationship investments made by both sides can help to identify those that generate ROI and those that have become 'stranded' (under-used or wasted). A shake-up will focus the parties on uncovering new opportunities. It is not advisable that key stakeholders or boundary personnel are changed or moved on. Such movements would be seen as an indication of likely partnership dissolution by the Rebellious Teenager. Personnel changes in such instances can only be engineered through 'common consent' or when disagreements become too frequent.

Managing Evolving Pessimists

Evolving Pessimists continue to be difficult relationships despite the faint acceptance that 'something must be done'. The introduction of something new or different can potentially break the cycle of bad feelings and low productivity. These might include the arrival of a senior member of staff who has not been steeped in the old culture and does not bear the scars and unpalatable memories of the past, or a significant business opportunity that re-establishes collaboration and optimism. To succeed, these events need to be sufficiently hard-hitting to intrude into the preoccupation of both partners on their external problems and force them to devote some effort to managing their key relationship. In the Chapter 7 case study, the supplier key account manager appealed to a faction within the relationship – the engineers – and used their natural affinity to build bridges between the firms. Against some opposition from his board, who felt that any investment in the relationship would not be reciprocated, he made changes to his customer support organization to demonstrate a new commitment to service.

Within Evolving Pessimist relationships, trust between the partners may be very thin on the ground and unilateral action is needed to break the impasse. Perhaps there is a natural point when poor quality relationships are so 'battle-weary' that they become open to the suggestion of change. Thus, if either side chooses the right time to offer carefully targeted measures, they may stand a fair chance of success, although initially they are likely to be viewed with some suspicion by the other party and possibly by their own staff as well.

Due to the continued environmental situations faced by the companies, it is likely that any relationship performance improvement will take time and continued, determined effort and political pressure to work. Nevertheless, once these improvements take hold, they may gain a momentum of their own.

Managing Captive Sharks

The first rule is that Captive Sharks cannot be managed; the second is they can be understood and partially tamed. The importance of the relationship to the parties involved can be immediately obvious, and this often masks any exploration of why it is important and what are the markers of success for the parties concerned. Typically, in most Captive Shark relationships there is a naïve understanding of the business models of the parties involved. Senior VPs can often be heard bemoaning the fact that their partner 'simply does not understand our business', but when asked if they understand their partner's business, no answer is forthcoming. This leads on to areas of aggravation. The business model that drives one party to encourage its partner to invest in the partnership can be a radically different model to the other, which sees the investment as a necessity rather than an opportunity.

Captive Shark relationships are discernible between large manufacturers and large retail outlets as well as between raw material suppliers and power-generating companies. Both parties are 'hostage' to the relationship, which is a necessity for the success of their business. However, neither is willing to move away from the 'win-lose' negotiating position to look for common advantage.

Captive Sharks can be tamed by understanding the motivations (positive and negative) of the partners in sustaining the relationship (the strategic logic) and understanding the mechanisms or model by which success will be measured (critical success factors). This can only come about through dialogue, which needs to start at the top of the organization and, in many respects, is akin to the initiation of a cultural change programme, ie recognizing the need to change. Inter-organizational learning will support this change and also enable the parties to understand the commercial, cultural and administrative processes of their partner. It also helps them to adopt and adapt modes of operation that are sympathetic to the partnership rather than wholly self-centred.

As such relationships mature, then their developmental path can move them closer to Stable Pragmatists, which can learn to innovate collectively and cooperate effectively. Captive Shark relationships rarely terminate peacefully; litigation is an obvious risk, but typically it is the change in market position of one of the partners that alters the economic value, and results in a very quick evaporation of commitment.

Managing Cherry Pickers

While Cherry Pickers can often represent a major opportunity, the ability to convert them into a more productive partner is not easy and requires considerable effort. Their lack of commitment is driven mainly by the Cherry Picker seeing little differentiation or incremental value in the relationship compared to other actual or prospective relationships. This translates into the firm seeing no value in investing in the partnership and the absence of a 'stake in the game' reinforces the lack of commitment. It is therefore important that the strategic logic or rationale for the partnership be explored and expanded such that the Cherry Picker is brought into the alliance. Normally the way to accomplish this is to embark on a series of executive-level discussions that open up ideas and opportunities; this will not be effective for Cherry Pickers, which would question the value of such an activity and the use of their time. Instead, one needs to approach Cherry Pickers as if they were being recruited into the partnership for the very first time, and usually this can be done without too much difficulty.

The re-engagement can start by exploring the strategic reasons for both partners to work together, a critical examination of the value proposition that the host firm brings to the table, and an appraisal of the strengths and weaknesses of collaboration. Once agreement on these points is achieved, the partners can then turn to the practical issue of how to manage the relationship more effectively. If this process then addresses a specific commercial opportunity such as a major tender, real progress can be made in integrating the Cherry Picker into the partnership. Thus by concentrating the Cherry Picker on a single activity, a single customer or single process, it can be possible to raise its expectation level and open the way to broadening the relationship in the future.

Managing No Can Dos

No Can Do relationships will often occur because difficult operating conditions such as highly uncertain markets, complex technical challenges and problematic political or economic conditions force relationships to turn inward on themselves. The cumulative build-up of dissatisfaction due to perceived 'injustices' then leads to worsening relationship behaviours. This process can take a number of years to mature and in consequence the adversarial behaviours become embedded in the culture and are extremely hard to shift. It is thus likely that simple indoctrination programmes, even if wholeheartedly backed by senior management, will fail and more radical strategies will be needed. In the UK, the automobile industry of the 1970s and 1980s had become so uncompetitive that wholesale restructuring was the only solution.

In the MoD, for example, the change programme has been progressing for over 10 years and to date has probably only achieved about 65 per cent of its objectives. It included the initial production of a comprehensive new doctrine on partnering backed by training and management development. The creation of over 100 joint integrated project teams together with a series of extensive reorganizations, relocations and the building of expensive new office complexes, was designed to facilitate the changes. The MoD's financial systems were completely reorganized on more commercial lines, and considerable efforts began to involve the military end-customers in the process of procuring and supporting weapons systems. In its turn, industry has been driven by increasing costs and competition to rationalize through acquisition (there is now a fraction of the number of defence companies there was 10 years ago) and to streamline its operations into fewer sites with considerably fewer staff. It has, moreover, gradually moved away from its traditional 'take it or leave it' position and is very slowly accepting the responsibilities of joint working.

A UK-based, major logistics company recently faced the difficult challenge of changing its stalled culture and that of its network of partner companies to enable it to expand into Europe or succumb to a hostile takeover. Many of the management and staff in these relationships were either unable or unwilling to change: No Can Dos. Senior managers decided that there was neither the time nor the money to re-engineer the relationships quickly. They therefore closed the main company, terminated its partnering contracts, carried out a management buy-out and entered the market for fresh partners, giving preference to any previous partners who were prepared to change. In three years the company has become a major player in Europe and is looking for further expansion.

Within these massive upheavals, gradually, through the efforts of individuals and small teams and by means of small projects and initiatives, confidence and trust have been rebuilt and the old cycles of bad behaviour have been broken. Given the size of the organizations, progress has been slow and not uniform, but it can be shown that culture can change and a transition to Stable Pragmatist may take place.

Managing Deserters

The most critical decision is whether a Deserter relationship is actually worth the investment of time and energy. Many Deserters can represent low levels of commercial value and it is questionable whether promoting the partnership is justifiable. On the other hand, where a valuable partnership does display Deserter tendencies, it is important to consider actions carefully.

The root cause of many such situations is the lack of expected operational performance. It is thus critically important to understand the joint expectation levels and then instil a sense of reality. The next step is to develop clearly defined actions to achieve a particular short-term objective that brings tangible benefits and demonstrates to the Deserter the advantages of continuing in the partnership. A possibility is to change personnel to create a fresh approach, perhaps replacing the incumbent account or alliance manager or installing a new ambassadorial manager; this may get the Deserter's attention. The important point is that the new manager (having addressed outstanding queries and complaints) treats the relationship as if it were a new partnership. This requires a longer-term orientation to the development of the relationship and as such it is not unusual for a six to 12 month period to elapse before new, fresher and more positive perspectives are in place.

In large, complex alliances or supply chain partnerships, the change process can be far more protracted. Where many stakeholders are involved on both sides, changing a leading or coordinating manager is unlikely to have an immediate or significant impact. In fact experience suggests that in such situations the new manager is over-burdened very quickly with the issues and can become very disenchanted with his or her responsibilities, to the extent that he or she tends to move on to new positions and roles before the relationship is fully turned around. Unless there is a particular manager or individual who is the focus of complaints and concerns, it is better to maintain the alliance team but to step up the level of senior manager engagement. This figurehead must give the partnership the time and energy it requires to avoid accusations of 'lip-service' and ineffectiveness.

The Gibbs+Humphries Partnership Types and marketing

The account management of partnerships is obviously very important. In many situations, especially in marketing channels, significant time and money is spent in the development and execution of marketing programmes. Each of the eight relationship types has its own perceptions of the strength of the partnership in terms of the following marketing parameters:

- communication;
- service or product competitiveness;
- brand value or reputation of the partner;
- profitability/margin;
- marketing cooperation support.

Table 8.4 Target partners' relative evaluation of key marketing factors

Type	Communication	Competitiveness	Brand	Profitability	Support
Evangelists	Excellent	Excellent	Excellent	Excellent	Excellent
Stable Pragmatists	Good	Good	Good	Moderate	Good to Excellent
Captive Sharks	Poor	Moderate	Moderate	Poor	Poor
Rebellious Teenagers	Moderate	Moderate	Good	Moderate	Moderate to Good
Evolving Pessimists	Moderate to Poor	Moderate	Moderate	Moderate	Moderate
Cherry Pickers	Moderate	Moderate	Moderate to Good	Moderate	Moderate
No Can Dos	Poor to Moderate	Poor to Moderate	Poor to Moderate	Poor to Moderate	Poor to Moderate
Deserters	Very Poor	Very Poor	Very Poor	Very Poor	Very Poor

An assessment of how each is viewed by the individual Gibbs+ Humphries Partnership Types will impact on the effectiveness and suitability of marketing messages. Table 8.4 sets out the key factors that influence this activity.

Evangelists

Typically there is no such thing as over-communication for an Evangelist, as long as it is a message that it is familiar and comfortable with. Consistent reiteration of conservative messages reinforcing the established values of the brand and product competitiveness are preferred. The Evangelist will be less comfortable with the introduction of new processes and procedures or sudden changes of direction. There is a view that the level of investment directed towards Evangelists can be reduced as their level of commitment is sufficiently high and the need to overcome any inertia is low. Nevertheless, periodically it is important to inject new capital into the enterprise to keep it on track, and in marketing channels this means being prepared to provide marketing and sales support to ensure that the partner is not adversely affected by changing events. Evangelists are by default very loyal and will always speak well of their partnership, which has a beneficial effect on the industry and the financial markets.

Stable Pragmatists

The key difference between Evangelists and Stable Pragmatists is the pragmatic view of the latter. Stable Pragmatists are very satisfied with all aspects of the marketing mix and do not 'waste time' effusing over the partnership. They are nevertheless particularly impressed with the level of support (both sales and marketing) that they receive from their partner.

Captive Sharks and Rebellious Teenagers

The business models of Captive Sharks, and to some extent Rebellious Teenagers, is an area where the greatest level of misunderstanding normally exists. For both types of relationship it is important that frequent reviews are undertaken so that the impact of changed market conditions, new policies or market initiatives is sympathetic to the commercial needs of the partner.

The Novell case study in Chapter 3 provides an illustration of this point. The acquisition of the consultancy firm by Novell created conflict with the partners simply because the initiative threatened their service and support revenue and changed their business model from box-based margins to a client service model. A lack of appreciation of the evolving business model of partners can be a major cause for relationship difficulties. Generally the one area that the Captive Shark will recognize as having some merit is the brand value of the partner and the extent to which the brand represents a positive reputation and credibility.

Rebellious Teenagers are often concerned with the ongoing competitiveness of the focal product or service. They believe that the product may start to lack the technical or cost advantage that made it an attractive proposition in the past. Firms should consider how their communication to the partner can overcome any latent concerns on either immediate or anticipated market positioning. The publication of technical and strategic white papers, either into the public domain or under non-disclosure arrangements, can be a viable tactic to rekindle the partner's confidence in the host firm's credibility and competencies.

Captive Sharks are far more sceptical and cynical of such tactics and will probably be more responsive to direct messages on the commercial value of the business relationship, the level of investment that the host has made, and the return on investment that the partner can enjoy. Captives Sharks will be more responsive to direct discussions on the strength and dynamics of the business model and how they can increase their perceived low level of ROI. Such joint planning sessions will often be stressful, but can nevertheless lead to new, creative initiatives being undertaken. Where the Rebellious Teenager is concerned about the ongoing profitability of the relationship, the Captive Shark has already come to the conclusion that the business model is broken.

Cherry Pickers

The marketing approach to Cherry Pickers should be aimed at driving up their level of dependency on the brand, which they already hold in some esteem. They require convincing of the benefits of the fuller product portfolio. Firms should consider how they can increase their partners' understanding and appreciation of the strength of the brand (the firm's skills and competences and overall position in the market) and the functional capabilities of the full range of products. In marketing channels, authorization and accreditation programmes can be very successful in driving the increase in commitment from Cherry Pickers to the host firm.

No Can Dos

No Can Dos are reminiscent of Cherry Pickers except that they are less receptive to marketing messages. Nevertheless, effort can be usefully directed at re-establishing the basic value proposition of brand, product and profit.

Deserters

There is an argument that all efforts in marketing will fail with Deserters. They are no longer cynical like the Captive Sharks or seeking reassurance as the Rebellious Teenager. Deserters tend to be antagonistic; as such, generalist marketing initiatives can be doomed to failure. Experience suggests that one-to-one marketing and account management activities can be successful in re-energizing a Deserter. The critical caveat is the relative value to the partnership compared to the cost of management and motivation.

Conclusion

This final chapter has drawn together the numerous theoretical, strategic and operational ideals and concepts that have been discussed in previous chapters. It has explored in greater detail some of the background implications of the different Gibbs+Humphries Partnership Types. It has looked at practical ways in which an alliance, channel or partnership manager can proactively improve the level of relationship quality with its strategically important partners and visualize how such efforts can produce immediate and lasting effects on business performance. Significantly, it can be shown that improvements in the level of relationship quality can be achieved over a relatively short period of time and that tangible benefits can be enjoyed as a consequence. There are examples of firms moving from a parity position to a lead ranking within 18 months. Finally, this chapter has shown how the ability to objectively assess the relationship performance factors that drive commercial partnerships and alliances is not rocket science and should be useable by all 'thinking managers'.

Key action points

1. Consider your strategic alliance or other top five partners and try to determine their relationship type by applying the exercises described in this chapter.

2. Review your existing account, channel or relationship management strategies and determine how they improve the level of relationship performance.

3. Review your existing account, channel or relationship management strategies and determine whether they reflect a generalist view to your partners or whether you reflect their specific relationship needs.

4. Identify a product or service and consider how your sales and marketing might be improved by recognition of the prevalence of specific G+H Partnership Types.

5. Undertake an audit of your marketing activities and determine how each initiative or programme creates or diminishes the level of relationship performance overall.

Further reading

Brennan, R, Canning, L E and McDowell, R (2007) *Business-to-Business Marketing*, SAGE Advanced Marketing Series, London

Christopher, M (2005) *Logistics and Supply Chain Management: Creating value-added networks*, 3rd edn, FT Prentice Hall, Oxford

Christopher, M and McDonald, M (2003) *Marketing: A complete guide*, Palgrave Macmillan, Basingstoke

Coughlan, A T, Anderson, E and Stern, L W (2007) *Marketing Channels*, 6th edn, Prentice Hall International Series, Oxford

Cousins, P, Lamming, R, Lawson, B and Squire B (2007) *Strategic Supply Management: Principles, theories and practice*, FT Prentice Hall, Oxford

Davis, E W and Spekman, R E (2003) *The Extended Enterprise: Gaining competitive advantage through collaborative supply chains*, FT Prentice Hall, Oxford

Doz, Y L and Hamel, G (1998) *Alliance Advantage: The art of creating value through partnering*, Harvard Business Press, Boston MA

Dyer, J H, Kale, P and Singh, H (2001) How to make strategic alliances work, *MIT Sloan Management Review*, **42,** (4), pp 37–431

Gattorna, J (2006) *Living Supply Chains: How to mobilize the enterprise around delivering what your customers want*, FT Prentice Hall, Oxford

Hines, P, Found, P, Griffiths, G, Harrison, R (2008) *Staying Lean: Thriving, not just surviving*, Cardiff University Press, Cardiff

Kotler, P and Keller, K L (2006) *Marketing Management*, 12th edn, Prentice Hall of India, Delhi

MacBeth, D K and Ferguson, N (1994) *Partnership Sourcing: An integrated supply chain management approach*, Financial Times, London

McDonald, M (2007) *Malcolm McDonald on Marketing Planning: Understanding marketing plans and strategy,* 3rd edn, Kogan Page, London

Porter, M E (2004) *Competitive Strategy: Techniques for analyzing industries and competitors,* Free Press, New York

Rackham, N, Friedman, L and Ruff, R (1995) *Getting Partnering Right: How market leaders are creating long-term competitive advantage,* McGraw-Hill, Maidenhead

Ryals, L and Humphries, A S (2007–8) Seeing eye to eye, *Chief Purchasing Officers' Agenda,* **3,** (4)

Senge, P (2006) *The Fifth Discipline: The art and practice of the learning organization,* Doubleday, New York

Stock J R and Lambert, D (2001) *Strategic Logistics Management,* McGraw-Hill, Maidenhead

Williamson, O E (1999) *The Mechanisms of Governance* Oxford University Press, Oxford

Index

ALSO AVAILABLE FROM KOGAN PAGE

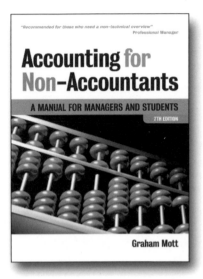

ISBN: 978 0 7494 5264 3 Paperback 2008

Accounting for Non-Accountants

A Manual for Managers and Students
7th Edition
Graham Mott

"A good introduction to the basics of accounting and business finance in an easy-to-follow style."
Business Executive

Now in its seventh edition, *Accounting for Non-Accountants* is widely used as an introductory text for business and management students on a variety of courses, and it remains essential reading for anyone wishing to truly understand accounting principles and practice.

ISBN: 978 0 7494 5318 3 Hardback 2008

The Innovation Handbook

How to Develop, Manage and Protect your Most Profitable Ideas
Adam Jolly

The Innovation Handbook is designed as a practical guide to the effective management of ideas for future leaders who want to move ahead of their competitors and offer new sources of value to their customers.

Drawing on a wide range of experience and expertise in strategy, technology, brands, intellectual property, finance, marketing and management, it will enable you to consider how best to combine an open search for potential winners with a process that captures their full value.

Order online now at www.koganpage.com

Sign up for regular e-mail updates on new
Kogan Page books in your interest area

ALSO AVAILABLE FROM KOGAN PAGE

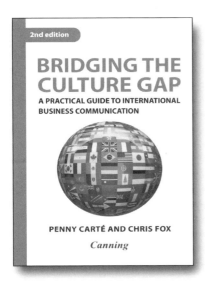

ISBN: 978 0 7494 5274 2 Paperback 2008

Bridging the Culture Gap

A Practical Guide to International Business
Communication
Penny Carté and Chris Fox

Bridging the Culture Gap will help you to become a better
communicator in any multicultural situation.

Packed with fascinating cases, cultural awareness scales,
communication style tests and practical tips, this lively
guide will help anyone – of any nationality – to become a
better communicator. Whether you're planning to give a
presentation to a cross-cultural group or about to negotiate
with an overseas client, *Bridging the Culture Gap* will ensure
that your cultural awareness antennae are well tuned.

ISBN: 978 0 7494 5231 5 Paperback 2008

The Business Plan Workbook

The Definitive Guide to Researching, Writing up and
Presenting a Winning Plan
6th Edition
Colin Barrow, Paul Barrow and Robert Brown

"Highly informative and instructive."
City Business Magazine

The Business Plan Workbook has established itself as the
essential guide to all aspects of business planning. Based
on methodology developed at Cranfield School of
Management and using successful real-life business plans,
The Business Plan Workbook brings together the process
and procedures required to help you produce that
persuasive plan.

Order online now at www.koganpage.com

Sign up for regular e-mail updates on new
Kogan Page books in your interest area

ALSO AVAILABLE FROM KOGAN PAGE

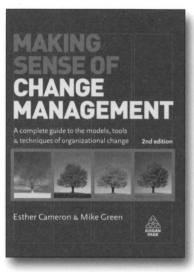

ISBN: 978 0 7494 5310 7 Paperback 2009

Making Sense of Change Management
A Complete Guide to the Models, Tools and Techniques of Organizational Change
2nd Edition
Esther Cameron and Mike Green

"This impressive book on change is an essential read for any professional manager who is serious about getting to grips with the important issues of making change happen."
Dr. Jeff Watkins, MSc Course Director, University of Bristol, UK

Making Sense of Change Management identifies and gives explanations of all current models of change, as well as offering practical guidelines and examples to show you why change can go wrong and how to get it right.

ISBN: 978 0 7494 4507 2 Paperback 2007

Change Management Masterclass
A Step by Step Guide to Successful Change Management
Mike Green

"Provokes thought and reflection...Anyone about to embark on, or already in the process of change, should read this book. It is well written, well researched, and ties in academic work on the subject nicely into real-life case studies."
Manager

Change Management Masterclass explains the process in clear terms. It looks at why organizations need to change, the different ways in which change can be approached and what makes a process of change management successful. It analyzes the process in a structured way to help you understand the concepts and deal with the challenges that arise.

Order online now at www.koganpage.com
Sign up for regular e-mail updates on new
Kogan Page books in your interest area

ALSO AVAILABLE FROM KOGAN PAGE

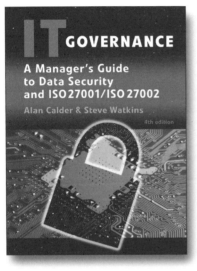

ISBN: 978 0 7494 5271 1 Paperback 2008

IT Governance
A Manager's Guide to Data Security and ISO 27001 / ISO 27002
4th Edition
Alan Calder and Steve Watkins

IT Governance examines standards of best practice for the protection and enhancement of information security management systems, allowing you to ensure that your IT security strategies are co-ordinated, coherent, comprehensive and cost effective. Each book comes with password-protected access to the www.itgovernance.co.uk website, for the latest news updates in this dynamic and constantly changing sector.

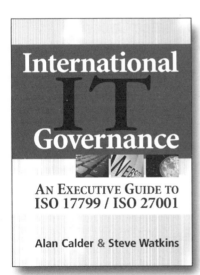

ISBN: 978 0 7494 4748 9 Paperback 2006

International IT Governance
An Executive Guide to ISO 17799/ISO 27001
Alan Calder

"A definitive guide to new legislation and practice for information security professionals and executives with an interest in business, regulatory compliance and IT management."
Abstracts of Public Administration, Development and the Environment

International IT Governance enables you to understand best practice in dealing with information security risks. The book is an essential guide to the new legislation for forward-looking future managers.

ALSO AVAILABLE FROM KOGAN PAGE

ISBN: 978 0 7494 5449 4 Hardback 2009

Managing Business Risk

A Practical Guide to Protecting Your Business
6th Edition
Jonathan Reuvid

"An impressive collection of articles and essays giving best practice advice on all aspects of managing risk."
Manager

Effective risk management is a vital issue for any company wishing to safeguard its commercial future.

Managing Business Risk reveals how to maintain the clearest possible controls on risks and deliver transparent reporting to stakeholders, drawing on expert advice from leading risk consultants, lawyers and regulatory authorities.

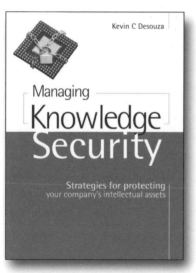

ISBN: 978 0 7494 4961 2 Hardback 2007

Managing Knowledge Security

Strategies for Protecting Your Company's Intellectual Assets
Kevin C Desouza

"Intellectual assets will form the basis for wealth creation...
Managing Knowledge Security *is concerned with the disciplines of managing and protecting these intellectual assets."*
CIPD Journal

Citing international examples such as Hewlett Packard, Microsoft, Google, Boeing and Amazon, *Managing Knowledge Security* covers all aspects of knowledge protection from employee retention strategies, to physical security and crisis management. It stresses the importance of taking measures to retain key assets and to avoid data and knowledge falling into the hands of competitors, plus includes practical strategies based on the author's own field experience.

Order online now at www.koganpage.com

Sign up for regular e-mail updates on new
Kogan Page books in your interest area

ALSO AVAILABLE FROM KOGAN PAGE

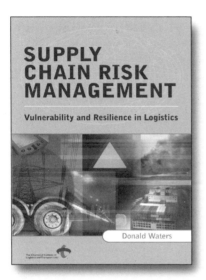

ISBN: 978 0 7494 4854 7 Hardback 2007

Supply Chain Risk Management
Vulnerability and Resilience in Logistics
Donald Waters

"Comprehensive coverage of the important areas of managing supply chain risk."
Professor Alan Waller, President of the Chartered Institute of Logistics and Transport, UK

Vulnerability to sudden supply chain disruption is one of the major threats facing companies today. *Supply Chain Risk Management* reviews the current thinking on identifying, analysing and responding to risk, describes the most widely used methods, and shows where the subject is heading.

It is essential reading for students who need to know about risk management and its growing impact on the supply chain.

ISBN: 978 0 7494 4945 2 Hardback 2007

Managing Risk in Extreme Environments
Front-line Business Lessons for Corporates & Financial Institutions
Duncan Martin

"All risk professionals, whatever their field, would benefit from reading this book."
Dr Chris Marrison, founder and CEO, Risk Integrated LLC

Managing Risk in Extreme Environments looks at real-life examples – from epidemics to earthquakes – to showcase risk management strategies which have been tested in adverse conditions and shown to succeed. The author then demonstrates how the lessons learnt from each can be effectively applied in future business scenarios.

ALSO AVAILABLE FROM KOGAN PAGE

ISBN: 978 0 7494 4984 1 Paperback 2007

The Handbook of Project Management
A Practical Guide to Effective Policies,
Techniques and Processes
Revised 2nd Edition
Trevor L Young

"A practical, comprehensive guide to be used frequently."
Euronet

The Handbook of Project Management will help students
acquire the basic tools and techniques for managing
projects in the real world. The book is accompanied by a
CD ROM containing a collection of tools, templates and
procedures which support the methodology used.

ISBN: 978 0 7494 5010 6 Hardback 2007

Project Management Survival
A Practical Guide to Leading, Managing and Delivering
Challenging Projects
Richard Jones

*"What's useful about this book is that it assumes that most
projects have already gone wrong before they're off the ground
and that resources and times are not just limited, but
inadequate – welcome to real world project management."*
CNBC European Business

This book provides business students with a template for
success based on tried and tested project management
techniques. The author shows them how to avoid project
killers and also gives practical advice on getting to the heart
of a project, getting the right initial plan, and developing a
genuinely workable plan. Importantly, he also discusses
how to manage people so the project stays on track.

Order online now at www.koganpage.com
Sign up for regular e-mail updates on new
Kogan Page books in your interest area

ALSO AVAILABLE FROM KOGAN PAGE

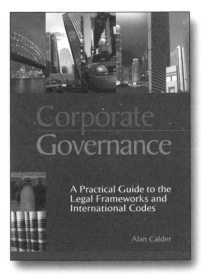

ISBN: 978 0 7494 4817 2 Hardback 2008

Corporate Governance
A Practical Guide to the Legal Frameworks and International Codes of Practice
Alan Calder

Corporate Governance will help you to become familiar with the principles and practice of good governance, showing you how to uphold those standards that will improve corporate reputation while providing reassurance to market regulators.

For future company directors, this is essential reading, and will answer all your questions on what good corporate governance means for a company's reputation and its share price.

ISBN: 978 0 7494 5085 4 Paperback 2008

The New Strategic Brand Management
Creating and Sustaining Brand Equity Long Term
4th Edition
Jean-Noel Kapferer

"Kapferer's book is one of the cornerstones of brand management in MBA programs today."
Anand P Rarnan, Senior Editor, Harvard Business Review"

Adopted internationally by business schools, MBA programmes and marketing practitioners alike, *The New Strategic Brand Management* is simply *the* reference source for senior strategists, positioning professionals and postgraduate students. Over the years it has not only established a reputation as one of the leading works on brand strategy but also has become synonymous with the topic itself.

Order online now at www.koganpage.com
Sign up for regular e-mail updates on new Kogan Page books in your interest area

www.koganpage.com

One website.

A thousand solutions.